In Real

D0622901

THE SOAP OPERA

The SAGE COMMTEXT Series

Editor:
F. GERALD KLINE
Director, School of Journalism and Mass Communication
University of Minnesota

Associate Editor:
SUSAN H. EVANS
Annenberg School of Communications,
University of Southern California

This new series of communication textbooks is designed to provide a modular approach to teaching in this rapidly changing area. The explosion of concepts, methodologies, levels of analysis, and philosophical perspectives has put heavy demands on teaching undergraduates and graduates alike; it is our intent to choose the most solidly argued of these to make them available for students and teachers. The addition of new titles in the COMMTEXT series as well as the presentation of new and diverse authors will be a continuing effort on our part to reflect change in this scholarly area.

—F.G.K. and S.H.E.

Muriel G. Cantor

Suzanne Pingree

THE
SOAP
OPERA

Volume 12. The Sage COMMTEXT Series

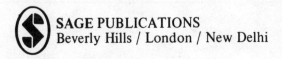

SAGE PUBLICATIONS
Beverly Hills / London / New Delhi

For information address:

SAGE Publications, Inc.
275 South Beverly Drive
Beverly Hills, Caiifornia 90212

SAGE Publications India Pvt. Ltd.
C-236 Defence Colony
New Delhi 110 024, India

SAGE Publications Ltd
28 Banner Street
London EC1Y 8QE, England

Printed in the United States of America

Library of Congress Cataloging in Publication Data

International Standard Book No. 0-8039-2004-0
                         0-8039-2005-9 (pbk.)
Library of Congress Card Catalog No. 83-11057

FIRST PRINTING

CONTENTS

PREFACE

This book has been in progress for several years. Our purpose in writing it should be obvious from the contents. Both of us have been teaching courses on women and the media for at least five years and, working independently, we came to similar realizations. Long ignored as a serious topic for research, soap operas are nevertheless the most profitable programs on the air. Throughout the book, we show the importance of the soaps to broadcasters, to advertisers, and to certain segments of the audience. In a brief overview of the history, production, contents, and audiences, we alert students and others to the complexities of the genre and its effects, and to the possibilities of further research.

The book is a joint enterprise, with the labor divided according to our respective areas of interest and expertise. Muriel Cantor wrote the chapter on production, most of the historical material, and the conclusion; Suzanne Pingree wrote the chapter on *The Guiding Light*, most of the content chapter, and those sections of the audience chapter dealing with uses and gratifications, and effects. The other chapters were written jointly. We also edited and critically reviewed each other's work.

It is important to acknowledge those who helped us. We are particularly grateful to Lucy Antek Johnson, head of daytime television for NBC, to All Rabin, co-executive producer, and Beth Milstein, assistant producer, of *Days of Our Lives*, and to Robert Bowden of Paramount Pictures. Cantor interviewed Larry Keith, who played Nick Davis on *All My Children* in 1976 when he was also president of the New York Branch of the Screen Actors' Guild. His description of his role on that soap opera alerted her to the differences between prime-time and daytime production and contributed to the inquiry that led to this book.

Students in our classes who provided insights into their own viewing experiences cannot be individually thanked. However, at UCLA, where Cantor was a Visiting Professor in 1982, Cheryl Zollars assisted directly with editing and informed criticism. A number of ex-soap opera actors and writers whom Cantor interviewed, in addition to the observations at *Days of Our Lives*, provided the necessary information for the chapters on history and production. In particular, Irv and Tex Elman, who were head writers for *General Hospital*, were especially helpful. Cantor is also grateful to both the American University and to Communication Studies at UCLA for the year in California.

At the University of Wisconsin — Madison, Pingree has worked with over 300 undergraduates on soap opera research projects in her classes. Their enthusiasm and energy contributed qualitatively to our chapter on content. Graduate students Sandy Starrett, Donna Rouner, and Debra Mies helped with the conceptualization and analyses of Pingree's work, for which we are grateful. Dr. Susan O'Leary and Professor Diane Kravetz both provided critical commentary on the feminist implications of serials. Madelyn Ladner typed parts of the manuscript, often answering our call for copy with almost no notice at all.

Our husbands, Robert P. Hawkins and Joel M. Cantor, were both supportive and critical of the thinking and writing that went into this manuscript. We especially want to thank F. Gerald Kline and the people at Sage for their support and patience with the writing.

Soap operas are often ridiculed by critics and scholars, and many have been surprised when we tell them about this enterprise, curious as to whether such effort is worthwhile.

Of course, it has been. We learned that soap opera production is truly another world. History shows that as the world turns, so does its content. As scholars, we will continue to spend the days of our lives in re-search for tomorrow. It is not surprising that we dedicate this book to all our children: Murray Cantor in Texas, who has never watched a soap opera; Jim Cantor in the Capitol, who provided the guiding light in leading his mother to the soaps in 1972; Jane Cantor Shefler, who prefers *Love Boat* reruns; and Paisley, Ray, and Haley Pingree-Hawkins, who are still too young and restless to be soap opera fans.

1

INTRODUCTION

A brief review of the book, including its rationale, chapter outlines, and a note on methods.

This is a study of daytime serials (soap operas), which are broadcast in the afternoon over the three television networks five days a week, 52 weeks a year. Each day approximately 25 million people, more than 80 percent of them women, watch the daytime serials (World Almanac, 1982). Since the early 1930s, when the soap opera was first presented on national network radio, daytime serials have continued to engage viewers, maintaining their popularity throughout World War II and even after radio was supplanted by television. Many observers believed that the soap opera could not be transferred to television, but not only did the genre transfer easily, it prospered and grew during a time when the daytime audience, mostly housewives, was declining as more women entered the labor force.

Our purpose in writing this book is to integrate the soap opera into the field of mass communications. The soap opera is important as a form of popular culture and as an economic commodity, and in comparison to other kinds of television drama, it is unique. In its pure form, the soap opera is the only type of nationally televised dramatic entertainment specifically targeted by advertisers for the female audience, although some men watch regularly. Originally created for the housewife, it has remained a medium through which advertisers and commercial networks try to reach a specific audience. Those who create the programs are interested primarily in the women at home who are potential buyers of the products advertised during the shows, while other drama on television is produced with a more heterogeneous audience in mind.

Soap operas are dismissed by many as prime examples of the low-level, standardized fiction found on commercial television. By high-brow literary or dramatic standards, the soap opera does not qualify as "art." Nevertheless, it is not good research practice to ignore a genre in which so many participate each day and which the television networks consider so important to their profits. Rather than considering the artistic merits or demerits of the soaps, our purpose is to show how the content has changed over time and how the messages in the soaps differ from those found in prime-time drama, to examine the production process historically, and to show how audiences have changed as the position of women has changed. The soap opera provides an ideal example of a popular art form that has evolved to meet the changing social conditions of its followers.

The focus of this study will be the content and the audiences, but in order to understand them both, it is necessary to show how the programs are selected, disseminated, and received. The social and cultural contexts in which the programs are produced, the organizational milieu of production, the creative people responsible for the programs, and the relationship of the audience to the productive process will all be examined. In addition, how the shows affect the audience will also be considered.

Soap operas are distinguished from other television fare by their format and content (expressive elements), mode of production, and audiences. These differences will be documented throughout. In addition, the soap opera, though one of broadcasting's most stable program forms, itself has changed over time. Although these changes have not always been those desired by social action groups or critics, most can be related directly to changes in the larger social milieu. One of the paradoxes of popular culture as a whole is that although its content changes, the underlying messages remain conservative and rather traditional. By this we mean that most popular art forms, especially those transmitted through commercial television, tend to *follow* social change rather than *lead* it. Soap operas, like their prime-time counterparts, help to maintain social integration and value consensus, albeit imperfectly.

Although generally conservative (traditional) and standardized, not all popular cultural forms are monolithic in message. There are a variety of crosscurrents in American society, some of which may be at odds with each other. As a rule, soap operas tend to present very traditional views of the female world. Some, however, particularly those targeted to younger women, have experimented with volatile issues such as abortion, child abuse, and wife battering, all of which reflect society's changing concerns. In some cases the positions taken can even be considered "liberal." Other soap operas present few social issues but frequently show women working in nontraditional occupations. Thus, some soap operas have moved away from tradition in sexual aspects and the way they present social problems, while others have done so in the way they present women in the work and business worlds.

All soap operas present to national audiences views of social relationships and sexual intimacies. How these views "affect" the audience is a controversial question. Rose Goldsen (1977), for example, believes that soap operas trivialize emotions and feelings, and while David Cohn (1943) thought radio soap operas insulted women's intelligence, Kathryn Weibel (1977) has suggested that because men and women are treated more equally on the soaps than in other television drama, they may actually contribute to women's liberation. All agree that love, duty, family, and intimate relations are at the core of the soap opera world. What kind of a world-view the audience cultivates from these images is an important but neglected topic. Part of our purpose is to look specifically at soap characteristics and to suggest research possibilities in an effort to answer some of the controversial questions raised by both critics and defenders.

In summary, we shall address some fundamental questions about one kind of television program. Why are the soaps the way they are? What makes them unique as a serial form? How do they differ from other kinds of television entertainment? In what ways have they evolved and changed over the fifty years they have been broadcast? Who watches them, and has that audience changed? What impact have soap operas had on viewers' behavior, beliefs, attitudes, and knowledge? The data necessary to answer such questions definitively are not available. However, by raising questions and providing some answers, we hope to encourage more and similar research.

OUTLINE OF THE BOOK

Chapter 2 provides some useful definitions. "Soap opera" is defined as a daytime serial and thus does not include the prime-time programs that may resemble the soaps. "Women's culture" is defined, and the approach being used is further specified.

Chapter 3 contains a brief history of the soap opera on radio. The focus here is on the economic and social conditions under which the soap opera flourished and finally disappeared. The emphasis is on the role of the broadcasters and the advertisers who supported the radio soap opera. The role of important creators is also noted.

Chapter 4 explains the transfer of the soaps to television, starting in 1950, and their growth in the medium. Again, the role of broadcasters and advertisers is emphasized. Later in the chapter, the production process itself is described, showing how soaps have remained a broadcast medium whose future and past are directly connected to the fate of network television.

Chapter 5 focuses on content. Divided into two parts, the chapter first discusses in depth the soaps' portrayal of female culture, showing how sex, social issues and problems, illness and health are presented to viewers. It then examines the "dramatic demography," social status (as reflected in work and occupation), and sex role inequalities.

Chapter 6 contains original research — a content analysis of radio and television scripts of *The Guiding Light,* the only soap opera still on the air that was originally broadcast on radio and then continued on television. It is the longest-running network program being broadcast in the United States. This analysis emphasizes the differences between the radio and television programs and shows how social relations, involving both work and family, have changed during the past 35 years.

Chapter 7 is divided into three sections. The first describes the audience, both on radio and television, and how that audience has changed over time. The second examines the reasons that people watch and what types of gratification they receive from the soaps. The last section is a brief discussion of the research on soap opera effects. A different approach to research is suggested.

Chapter 8 contains a short summary and conclusions. The influence of the audience on a soap opera is explored, and the future of the soap opera is discussed in relationship to changing patterns of work and leisure.

A NOTE ON METHODS

The information for this book came from many sources, some of it from the popular press, both newspapers and magazines, but most from either social science research or original studies conducted especially for inclusion here. Given our long association with the media industries and our professional skepticism as researchers, the material from the popular press is used sparingly. We hope that a secondary benefit from this book will be to alert students to the incestuous relationships among the media. As a source of data, popular articles are often inaccurate and incomplete. More important, they are often "planted" to encourage soap opera viewing and to encourage the sales of the publications in which they appear. They frequently depend more on sensationalism than analysis. Other documentary sources such as trade publications *(Broadcasting, Variety,* and others) and reports from government agencies, such as the Federal Communications Commission, are more reliable and have been consulted throughout.

Original research appears in Chapters 5-7. We have also synthesized available research reports when appropriate. Students are encouraged to look at the original studies if they are interested in specific research techniques. Although we make no claim to its being all-inclusive, the bibliography should provide students with a useful guide for further research.

2

BACKGROUND

Definitions. For our purposes, soap operas include only the daytime dramas on the three commercial television networks, as distinguished from other kinds of serial drama which others call soaps, such as prime-time serials and mini-series. Provides an explanation and rationale for studying the soap opera and clarifies why we are focusing on daytime drama rather than all serial drama.

Despite their popularity for more than fifty years, until recently the daytime serials have not been taken seriously by media scholars and analysts. A few social scientists have now begun to study the soap opera along with other forms of popular culture (see Tegler, n.d.). Although the radio soap opera received some attention, soap operas on television, like other forms of television shown during the daytime hours, such as talk shows and quiz shows, were virtually ignored by social scientists and communication researchers until the 1970s. Even after 1970, only a few serious articles analyzing soap operas qualify as social science research.

Whereas prime-time television drama (Cantor, 1980, 1982), magazine fiction (Cantor and Jones, 1983), and popular music (Lewis, 1978) have been subject to inquiries from several theoretical perspectives, the soap opera has been studied only intermittently and atheoretically. Most serious studies are content analyses (see Chapter 5) and Natan Katzman's (1972) and Rose Goldsen's (1977) analyses are the only studies that try to explain the soap operas' continuing popularity within a contextual framework.

Although there are numerous articles on the soaps in the popular culture literature, the most widely cited and circulated books on the mass media reveal that daytime television in general, and soap operas in particular, are not considered part of the mass media. When mentioned at all, the soap opera is typically allocated but a paragraph or two. For example, George Comstock and his associates (1978), including Katzman, devote no more than a few pages to daytime television, and only a few paragraphs to soaps in their encyclopedic review of television. In another overview of broadcasting research, Elihu Katz (1977) provides a few references to daytime programming in the United States, but more to studies on news and prime-time programs. Melvin DeFleur and Sandra Ball-Rokeach (1982), who have written one of the most widely used texts for media students, do not mention the soap operas at all.

Media historians have also shown little interest in comparing the television soap opera with other types of media programs. Although radio historians recognize the importance of soap operas to broadcasting (for example, MacDonald, 1979), television historians do not. Most information on television soap operas is found in books devoted to serial drama or the topic of soap operas itself rather than in general discussions of television (see Edmondson and Rounds, 1973, 1976; LaGuardia, 1974; Stedman, 1977). In his three-volume history of broadcasting, Erik Barnouw (1966, 1968, 1970), the best-known broadcasting historian, devotes only a few pages to the radio soap opera and just one paragraph to the television daytime serial. In a later book (1975), Barnouw again wrote scantily on daytime television, with only one paragraph on the soap opera. This lack of attention is perplexing, because soaps are still a vital part of commercial broadcasting in America. In fact, no other program type has generated so much profit.

WHAT A SOAP OPERA IS

Soap operas are a form of serialized dramatic television broadcast daily over the three commercial television networks — American Broadcasting Company (ABC), National Broadcasting Company (NBC), and Columbia Broadcasting System (CBS), usually during the afternoon. These networks reach all the major marketing areas in the United States through approximately 600 affiliated stations. Together, the three networks' programming, all very similar, comprise the major source of news and entertainment for American viewers. As will be elaborated in the conclusion, the networks' hold on viewers is declining because of the adoption of new technology and changing patterns of work and leisure. However, the networks still attract approximately 80 percent of all viewers who use their television sets at one particular time of day.

During the mid-afternoon in most market areas, all three networks compete for viewers' time by showing serial dramas (soap operas). Soap operas are the only dramatic programming produced and video-taped daily, Monday through Friday, in broadcast studios shortly before they are aired. Networks broadcast a soap opera one week (or at the most two) after it is taped. Other dramas are usually video-taped (or filmed) several months before they are seen by the audience. Soap operas are shown throughout the year, five days a week, and are rarely preempted for other types of programming. That feature of soap operas makes them unique in comparison to other dramatic television. Only major news events, such as John Kennedy's assassination and the assassination attempts on Ronald Reagan and Pope John Paul, take precedence over the soaps.

Daytime television developed from daytime commercial radio, which had originated to reflect the interests of the advertisers' target audience, American housewives. Daytime radio's schedule was transferred almost intact to television in the early 1950s. At the height of their popularity on radio (1941-42), the beginning of a serial could be heard every quarter-hour between ten in the morning and six in the evening on one or more of the national radio networks (Stedman, 1977). Approximately 40 percent of all women listened to soap operas daily (Willey, 1961). Even during World War II, when many women entered the work force, the audience for soap operas remained large.

The Soap Opera and the Domestic Novel

Serialized drama as a form of entertainment was not new, though its form on radio was. In developing the soap opera, radio adapted one of literature's most enduring forms, the domestic novel (Stedman, 1977; Weibel, 1977). According to John Keeler (1980), the soap opera has much in common with the English sentimental novel, which originated in the eighteenth century. In *Pamela*, published in 1740 and considered by some to be the first modern novel, Samuel Richardson shows how a working "girl" (a house servant) struggles to act in accordance with her proper upbringing. After avoiding seduction, she marries her employer, a man with high social status. Although it is no longer required that heroines avoid seduction, that story is repeated over and over again in women's fiction, including soap operas.

Like so many of the novels that followed *Pamela*, soap opera stories are about ordinary people and the events of their daily lives. As in the English sentimental/domestic novel, characters in soap operas interact in a series of intertwined domestic or romantic melodramas.

There is much justification in associating the domestic novel, which was frequently presented in serial form, with the daytime radio serial. Both forms of "literature" were intended for female audiences. The stories were generally set in the present, rather than being historical, and most of the action occurred in domestic settings. Nineteenth-century domestic novels were written mostly by women, and more women were (and continue to be) involved in the creation and stories of daytime drama than any other broadcast programming (see Chapter 3).

Historians of the radio soap opera note that there were diverse types of serials on during the daytime hours. Raymond Stedman (1959: 58) lists the three "classes" of soap operas that were most common:

(1) The Woman Alone;

(2) The Problems of Marriage; and

(3) The Family Saga.

Although these three types, especially the latter two, are not mutually exclusive, they are useful for comparison. Stedman claims that the Woman Alone type was the most common, though this theme was not transferred to television, which sought serials focusing more on social relationships, especially between the sexes and among family members. The Woman Alone's underlying theme, of how a woman without a mate coped in a hostile world, has virtually disappeared. The Family Saga, structured around relationships involving two or three extended families, has prevailed.

The Woman Alone theme was quite common in the domestic novel. Nina Baym (1978) devotes her book to this theme in nineteenth-century women's fiction. She describes two different plots, both about a woman's survival without the external aids of family and husband. The heroine is either a poor orphan or a pampered heiress who becomes poor. Both show how the heroine develops the capacity to survive and surmount her troubles. The purpose of both plots is to deprive the heroine of all external aids and to make her success in life entirely a function of her own efforts and character (Baym, 1978: 35).

In radio serial after radio serial, as Stedman points out, a heroine faced the world alone. Sometimes the title revealed her situation. *Young Widder Brown, Girl Alone,* and *Portia Faces Life* are some examples. *Ma Perkins* and *The Romance of Helen Trent,* two of the most popular serials, were also about women coping without men, although sometimes seeking one.

The one known Woman Alone story for television, *Miss Susan,* was introduced in 1951 and lasted only a short time. In television, the Family Saga has been more successful, incorporating the problems of marriage and mate selection within a larger category. Television soap operas usually revolve around the relationships of two families and their associates. Single women characters are prevalent (for without them the genre would not exist), including family members, sweethearts, ex-wives, and potential lovers of family members. Of course, the soap opera has changed over the last fifty years. Still, the debt to the domestic novel remains. Characters presented in soap operas are easily identified as good or bad. Good characters are family-oriented and hold in check their ambitions and selfish desires. Work, although becoming more important than it has been in the past, is secondary to family ties. Only bad characters are openly seductive and aggressive in their careers. Soap operas have always been morality plays for women, whether Family Sagas or Women Alone stories (Keeler, 1980; Weibel, 1977; Cohn, 1943).

Form and Structure

The most obvious structural feature of daytime serials is that they never begin and never end. They are continuing stories, with competing and intertwining plot lines introduced as the serial progresses. Each plot on a given program develops at a different pace, thus preventing any clear resolution of conflict. The completion of one story generally leads into others, and ongoing plots often incorporate parts of semi-resolved conflicts.

Even when a soap opera is discontinued, story lines are not really ended. For example, *Love of Life,* broadcast on

American television from 1951 to the winter of 1980, simply went off the air. When new soap operas are introduced, they start in the middle, although sometimes they are spinoffs from other, more established soaps. NBC introduced *Texas* in 1980 using a main character from *Another World*, but otherwise it had no beginning.[1] *Capitol*, introduced in 1981, began in the middle of a crisis, with no transitional figures from another soap. The characters were involved in several stories, and the viewer had to unravel plot lines without help from a narrator or storyteller. For those who remember, radio listeners did have some help from the mellow tones of the announcers. Of course viewers of television soaps are aided by other, only slightly less obvious devices to ensure that everyone in the audience understands the plot.

One of these devices is the very slow pace of soap operas. Because the soaps were developed for the woman at home and continue to be produced primarily for women between 18 and 49 years who are home during the day, some have argued that the slow pace evolved to suit the needs of these women. Viewers/listeners are able to keep up with the plots and still take part in other activities, such as housework, shopping, and part-time paid or unpaid work. However, all soaps are not alike — not all are equally slow. In the newer ABC soaps, for example, events occur at two or three times the rate of CBS soaps, but even the faster soap operas are all much slower than real time or than prime-time television.

One feature related to the slow pace is the use of flashbacks, repetitious dialogue, and other devices to repeat vital information from day to day. These dramatic devices make it possible to miss weeks of episodes and still know enough of a story to resume viewing. It is almost impossible *not* to see a crucial scene, such as an accident or murder, on a soap; most are repeated numerous times in flashbacks after they are first broadcast. Also, for those who miss episodes, magazines such as *Soap Opera Digest* and some newspapers report the week's events.[2] Soap opera viewers also find out what is happening from their friends who watch. Thus, although there is a core group of daily soap opera viewers, many "fans" are able to be occasional viewers and still understand what is happening even after several weeks away from their sets.

Another characteristic of the soaps that distinguishes them from other serial drama is the paucity of action. What happens of soaps is usually told through conversation (dialogue) and not through the portrayal of events. There is little of the action-oriented, fast-moving violence so common in prime-time television. Television soaps are very similar to the old radio serials in this respect. Those who wish to can listen to the audio portion without even watching the television set and still understand the story fully. Because of their reliance on dialogue, television soap operas have been called "radio with pictures." That feature has made the programs popular with workers, who listen to them on FM radios while on the job, and among the blind (Liss, 1981).

WHAT A SOAP OPERA IS NOT

Although the serial form of drama has been very influential in giving mass entertainment its present form, not all serials qualify as soap operas. Serial drama is a natural format for the broadcasting media. An examination of television schedules worldwide reveals that various forms of serial drama comprise much entertainment programming. Serial drama has many advantages for both commercial and state broadcasters that other forms of dramatic entertainment do not. Its audiences are able to identify with and get to know the characters and to become involved with the stories. The serial format allows audience members to build a rapport with a character and/or an actor or actress in a particular role. Serials often provide the excitement of cliffhangers. Even if a cliffhanger is not a necessity, an engaging story is. Continuing stories bring viewers back for subsequent episodes.

The combination of story and actors provided by serial drama has proved to be successful in all societies and for all kinds of audiences wherever broadcasting exists. The forms of serial drama vary from society to society and from audience to audience within a society. Most serial dramas are not soap operas. Instead, they are closer in form to what has been called a "mini-series" in the United States. Such serials consist of a finite number of episodes which tell a story from beginning to end. Some, such as *Roots,* last for just five to ten hours of programming. Others, such as South American *telenovelas,* last for eight or nine months. Often these serials are novels adapted for television and some, especially those made in England and shown on public television in the United States, are considered culturally superior to the soap opera or soap opera-like serialized drama. In South America and other parts of the world the telenovela, produced locally by country, has been compared to the American soap opera but actually resembles the shorter series in form (Mejias-Rentas, 1982).

During the evening in the United States, both serials and episodic series are broadcast. Episodic series are made up of a number of complete stories, each revolving around a main character who appears in every segment. The episodic series has been the mainstay of American national prime-time network entertainment programming for more than twenty years (see Cantor, 1980). In the last five years, the serial format has been adapted to prime time. The term "soap opera" is used indiscriminately by media commentators. When popular with public television audiences in the 1970s, *The Forsyte Saga* was labeled a high-brow "soap opera." Presently *Dallas, Dynasty,* and other evening serials broadcast by the three commercial television networks are called "nighttime soaps." *Dallas* and its imitators and spinoffs have been compared to soap operas because they are serial drama. By our definition, however, these evening serials are not true soap operas, although their debt to daytime drama is easily recognized.

Evening or prime-time television dramas (serials and series) in the United States differ from the soap opera in three ways. Their production (costs and control), the number of episodes produced, and the content all distinguish teleplays from soap operas.

Both prime-time and daytime serials and series broadcast on radio were first produced by advertising agencies or sponsors. Today, evening shows are produced by independent companies, and most (except mini-series and movies made for television) are produced weekly (Cantor, 1980). Some 22 prime-time episodes are made each season, in contrast to approximately 250 episodes for network soap opera. Direct control of daytime serials has remained with the advertisers or with the network (FCC, 1980), while the production companies and the network now share control of prime time. Prime-time drama production cannot be distinguished from movie production. The same production companies that make prime-time drama also make motion pictures, and almost all films originally made for theater production are eventually shown on television. The soap opera has remained a broadcast medium, but with a different pace and different rules of production than those for prime time. Although many soap opera episodes are made each year, their production cost is relatively low compared to that of producing a prime-time series. Soap operas require fewer sets, and their production and creative personnel receive lower salaries. (We will elaborate on these points in Chapter 4.)

The most important difference between prime-time serials and series and daytime drama is in the content. On the surface, evening serials such as *Dallas* and *Dynasty* appear similar to the daytime soaps. Both emphasize sexual relations, especially adultery. The "morality" espoused in each series, however, is different. Daytime characters often give direct advice, such as: "Good people do not steal." More fundamental is the fact that prime-time serials deal with power and big business *(Knott's Landing* being an exception), as well as family and interpersonal relations. Blake

Carrington, one of the main characters of *Dynasty*, owns a large oil conglomerate. The Ewing family of *Dallas* also owns an oil company.

Another major difference is that prime-time serials contain more action than do soap operas. In one episode of *Dynasty*, Fallon Carrington (Blake's daughter) was in a car crash, had a premature baby, and found out that the man she thought was her real father was not. Meanwhile, her husband had an affair. That much action would last weeks in a daytime serial. Because the daytime serials evolve slowly each day, certain patterns have emerged. The crisis and action introduced on Fridays are usually resolved on Monday. Small crises occur on Wednesdays. In contrast, every prime-time episode is packed with many crises and resolutions.

All daytime serials qualify as manifestations of women's culture. Occasionally an adventure plot will be included in a soap opera, but most are "women's" stories, revolving around, love, duty, and family. Of course, prime-time serials are also about family. *Knott's Landing's* family problems and locale resemble a soap opera, but the two evening serials highest in ratings, *Dallas* and *Dynasty*, focus on power and money, as well as family and sexual relationships. Horace Newcomb (1981) compares *Dallas* to a western rather than a soap opera.

When appropriate, comparisons between the soap opera and prime-time drama are made throughout the book. We must emphasize, however, that the soap opera is unique in form and content. Although a soap opera could be broadcast in the evening, no prime-time show has ever qualified as a pure soap opera. *Peyton Place* (1964-1969) was probably the evening show most like a soap opera because of its themes and plots, but its pace was much more rapid. Norman Lear's *Mary Hartman, Mary Hartman* has also been called a soap opera (see Edmondson and Rounds, 1976; Craft, 1982), but it does not qualify by our definition either, because it mocked itself. Soap operas are serious, not satires, comedies, or parodies.

CONCLUSION

The soap opera, from its origin, has been and remains women's fiction. Of the various forms of fiction especially for women — such as Gothic and romance novels, including the popular Harlequin books, true confessions, photonovellas, magazine serials — the soap operas have had the largest continuing audience through time. Moreover, the soap opera in its pure form, as it is shown during the daytime hours, is the only type of national television drama targeted to a female audience. Although the number of women home during the day decreases every year as more American women enter the labor force, and although the number of male viewers increases as unemployment rises and men retire early, women are still the primary audience.

Advertisers and television networks are interested primarily in the consumers who buy the products being advertised, such as cleaning products and beauty aids. Women also comprise the majority of viewers in prime time as well as daytime, but during prime-time hours they are not nearly as large a majority — 52 percent of the audience, compared to 80 percent during the day. Most prime-time television is produced for a more sexually heterogeneous audience. In addition, from their beginning soap operas have often been created and written by women.

The content of a soap opera reflects its intended audience. The stories are women's stories, focusing on love, romance, childbearing, health and illness, manners and morals. The soap opera world is different from the world presented in prime time. Women's literature, in its more literary forms and those considered low-brow by critics, has been examined through its content (see Showalter, 1977, for one of many examples). There are also numerous content analyses of magazine fiction (Busby, 1975). These analyses are generally useful for showing how images and portrayals change or are perpetuated but not for showing how the context of production is related to the content (Cantor and Jones, 1983). Rather than simply doing another content analysis, here we are emphasizing the relationship of content to the social and economic contexts of production and transmission. We will show that societal factors such as norms and mores about women's place in the social order, as well as market conditions and the degree of government involvement, influence the content of soap operas more than individual values or the talent and creativity of the people responsible for the programs.

Although soap operas have had critics as well as defenders, soaps have not received as much critical scrutiny by social action groups, congressional committees, and government agencies as other forms of television drama. Most television criticism focuses on violence in prime-time and children's programs, and on how sex is portrayed in prime-time shows. Whether critics have influenced these shows is debatable (Comstock, 1982b), but there is no debate over the impact that social action groups have had on daytime television. The fact is, they have had no impact at all. Essentially, soap operas have been virtually ignored by such groups, except for a minor outcry by the Moral Majority in 1980 concerning sex. Powerful public action groups, such as the National Parent/Teacher Association, the American Medical Association, and Action for Children's Television, who have been working actively to change prime-time television and children's shows, do not seem to consider the soaps as part of national television.

Most critics of the soaps have attacked them for their lack of artistic merit or have questioned their psychological impact on female viewers. The most widely publicized criticism came from a psychiatrist, Louis Berg, who believed that soap operas pandered to perversity and caused anxiety, tachycardia, arithmias, increased blood pressure, profuse perspiration, and other negative symptoms (Stedman, 1959: 175).[3] His criticism and more recent ones have not concerned either the networks or advertisers because they have come from relatively powerless individuals (such as feminists) rather than from powerful public action groups. Because of that lack of concern, the soap opera has been free to evolve without interference. Part of the conservative nature of the soaps is due to the way in which creators and advertisers conceptualize the audience, and this may well account for the neglect of the soaps by action groups. Also, because government and private research funds have been limited, those who study television's effects have done little research on soap operas.

In this book we will look at the soap opera both historically and contemporarily, in order to shed some light on the questions raised in this chapter and the preceding one. We contend that all television programs are not alike, as some claim. Soap operas present a different message from other television drama; their history, mode of production, and possibly their effects are different as well.

The history of broadcasting in America and the history of soap operas are closely connected. To understand how television changes and how it affects viewers, it is inappropriate to ignore daytime programming in general and daytime serial drama in particular.

NOTES

1. *Texas* and *The Doctors* were broadcast for the last time on December 31, 1982. They also ended with stories unresolved. The following summaries were published in the *Los Angeles Times* (Reed, 1983): *Texas:* Since the show has no future, here's how it ended: Justin and Ashley reunited after she birthed a girl. Judith decided to give Grant and Reena a chance at happiness. Paige was optimistic that she and T. J. will have a future together. Brett was persuaded to take a job in Alaska. Allison and Ashley reconciled. Stella was promoted and Vicky threw a farewell party at KVIK after she lost ownership. And the only truly happy couple appeared to be Lurlene and Joel. *The Doctors:* Since the show has no future, here's how it ended: Jeff pulled the veil from his new bride who turned out to be Adrienne. Natalie was shocked to learn Paul and Felicia were arrested for murdering Billy. Matt and Maggie reconciled while Kit and Mike also planned a wedding. Althea got fed up with Jean Marc's preoccupation with Felicia.

2. There are at least ten such publications for soap fans, with *Soap Opera Digest* being the most circulated (Greenberg et al., 1982).

3. Berg's evidence for his claims were unscientific. He listened to several soaps and then took his own blood pressure. However, he was important because he led the anti-soap campaigns in the 1940s and is quoted by almost every book on soaps (Edmondson and Rounds, 1973; Thurber, 1948; Stedman, 1959, 1977).

3

SOAPS ON RADIO

A brief history of the soap opera on radio, focusing on the economic and social conditions under which the soap opera flourished and finally disappeared. Emphasis on the role of broadcasters and advertisers in supporting the radio soap opera. The role of important creators is noted.

This chapter is about the origins of the soap opera and its history on radio. The time period covered is from 1920, when radio first became a possibility as a mass medium, until 1960, when the last soap operas were discontinued on radio. This chapter is not meant to be a definitive history of radio serial drama. Others have written about radio generally, and the daytime serial in particular, in more depth than is possible here. (Further readings are suggested in the notes and references.)[1] Our emphasis is on the social and economic contexts in which the soap opera developed and prospered, but we do not ignore those responsible for creating the radio serial.

Studying the rise and fall of the radio soap opera, from the first network broadcast of *Betty and Bob* in 1932 to the last radio broadcast of six serials in November 1960, reveals that the radio serial greatly influenced the development of broadcasting, especially programming. Cultural forms of communication such as the radio soap opera changed in subtle but important ways as the social and economic conditions of production and reception changed.

Television soap opera fans are indebted to the companies that helped to originate and support the early shows. The soap opera flourished because manufacturers of soap and other household products were willing to experiment with an untried form of entertainment programming. As the female audience for serials grew during the 1930s, so did the number of programs. It was during the 1930s and 1940s that radio soap operas enjoyed their greatest success. During the 1950s, some soap operas were being broadcast on television as well, and network radio was beginning to lose its advertising support and audience to that medium. Thus, the history of the daytime serial is representative of the history of network broadcasting in the United States.

BACKGROUND

The soap opera as we know it would probably not have developed if broadcasting in the United States had not been supported by advertising. Although the serial form is an obvious and natural genre for any form of the mass media, it is especially well suited to a free enterprise system where sponsor support is necessary. The form that mass entertainment takes in any society depends fundamentally on the role of government in determining the regulatory and control mechanisms. According to law, the government is directly responsible for the organization and regulation of the broadcast industry in the United States. The establishment of commercial broadcasting, which permitted the selling of commercial time over the air, set the stage for the development of the soap opera.

From the beginning of radio broadcasting, the U.S. government established a regulatory role. The Radio Law of 1912 assigned to the Department of Commerce the authority to license experimental radio stations, but commercial broadcasting was not feasible until after World War I. The first radio station for a public audience went on the air in November 1920 as a venture of the Westinghouse Electric and Manufacturing Company. By July 1922, approximately 400 stations were licensed, and more were on the way. Newspapers were running columns and even whole sections on broadcasting. Many different enterprises were planning to open stations (Barnouw, 1978: 9). Throughout this growth period, controversy occurred over the proper source of financial support for radio broadcasting. That over-the-air broadcasting was to be primarily a commercial enterprise was unquestioned, but what form such commercial support would take remained unanswered during the first years.

In early 1922, AT&T announced that it would soon open a new kind of station, and eventually a nationwide chain of stations, to provide "toll broadcasting." These "radiotelephone" stations were compared to telephone booths. Anyone with the necessary fee could broadcast a message over the air in the same way one could telephone a friend. AT&T's proposal was not well received. Herbert Hoover, then Secretary of Commerce, said it was "inconceivable that we should allow so great a possibility for service [as radio] . . . to be drowned in advertising chatter." *Printer's Ink* thought that advertising would be "positively offensive to great numbers of people" (both quoted in Barnouw, 1978: 15). Nevertheless, AT&T opened WEAF (its first toll station) in August 1922. The growth of sponsorship and commercial radio continued despite criticism from intellectuals and educators.

In 1927, Congress passed the Radio Act, which created the Federal Radio Commission (FRC), later replaced by the Federal Communications Commission (FCC) after passage of the Communications Act in 1934. By 1927, commercial radio in the United States had become firmly established. The growing radio industry had asked for the creation of a regulatory body, though the Radio Commission's primary purpose was not to control programming, but rather to license stations. Thus, by 1927 the broadcast industry had achieved its present basic structure: a nationwide system of stations linked by telephone lines, local stations on temporary licenses, revenues from advertising, and a regulatory agency that by law

is to respect the rights of broadcasters under the First
Amendment to practice free speech while requiring broadcasters to base their decisions on the public interest, convenience, and necessity.

National Network Radio

In the early 1920s, radio broadcasting was primarily local.
Before the establishment of network radio, there were only
small, regional chains of stations, some bound by contract,
others teamed hastily for specific broadcasts. The National
Broadcasting Company (NBC) was established in 1926, the
Columbia Broadcasting System (CBS) in 1927. National radio
developed rapidly. By the end of the decade, both NBC and
CBS were sizable business enterprises, organized for profit
and able to provide sponsors with a national audience. NBC
was actually comprised of two networks (the "Red" and the
"Blue").[2] By 1930, NBC controlled 61 affiliates, and CBS controlled 79. Although scientific measures for determining audience size were undeveloped, the networks' combined
potential audience was known to be large. In 1929 alone,
4.4 million radio sets were sold (MacDonald, 1979: 27).

By 1930, the elements necessary for the development of
the soap opera were in place. Radio networks were able to
provide sponsors with a national audience and a clear signal.
Although radio was supposed to be programmed in the
public interest, according to government regulations the
term "public interest" had been applied only to programs
that were essentially noncommercial. The majority of program hours were available to be sold to sponsors for advertising products. However, sponsorship of network programs
during various time-slots and for different types of programming had not yet been determined. The story of the
soap opera (and of all other programming) after radio became a "mass medium" in 1930 is the story of American
manufacturers' need to find nationwide consumers for their

products, and of a few individuals' applied creativity and imagination in response to that need.

COMMERCIAL SPONSORSHIP OF RADIO PROGRAMS

During the 1927-1928 season, 39 companies sponsored programs for NBC, and 4 for CBS. In the following season, 65 nationally sponsored programs appeared on the air (Spaulding, 1979). Although all the time available to networks was not sold completely during the 1930s, in each year after 1928 the number of sponsored programs increased. At first, advertising agencies served the sponsors by preparing copy for broadcast in much the same way that they would later create and produce commercials for television. The networks, usually through the largest stations, supplied the programs to be sponsored, and as radio became more lucrative, advertising agencies became more important. Gradually, the large advertising agencies developed independent radio departments. At Ayers, one of the top advertising agencies, the radio department assembled information about all phases of broadcast advertising, built up programs, hired talent, directed production, and handled the leasing of the station time and all the other details connected with broadcast programs (Hower, 1949). Eventually, advertising production companies were completely responsible for radio programming.

Entire programs were developed, written, and packaged by various agencies. Potential sponsors decided whether to finance shows after viewing the final product. The advertising agency acted as a production company and provided the total package to a network. In addition, the agency sponsored the entire unit. The only function of the stations and the network was to provide the technical facilities through which to transmit the program.

The percentage of programs produced by advertising agencies grew quickly. In 1929, 33 percent of radio programming was produced by advertising agencies, 28 percent by the networks for sponsors, 20 percent solely by sponsors, and 10 percent by the so-called program builders (independent producers) (MacDonald, 1979). By 1937, the advertising agencies were producing mostly sponsored shows, and few, if any, new programs were aired that did not have sponsor support. Rather than working for the networks, actors, producers, writers, and even some announcers worked for the production companies that were owned by or subsidiaries of the advertising agencies.

Network soap operas, both on radio and television, have been described as the broadcast media's most profitable institution and have contributed heavily to the support of the major networks. Although soap operas were accepted slowly by the sponsors, by the end of their first decade they were generating more profit for the networks than any other program type.

Sponsorship of Daytime Serials

Radio programming changed radically between the late 1920s and the mid-1930s. Early network daytime radio was filled with pleasant but unspectacular shows, often providing American women with recipes and household hints. Locally produced dramatic shows were aired in the evening hours, especially in Chicago, and some stations were broadcasting serials. *Amos 'n' Andy* was the first daily serial to be broadcast in the evening by a network. Before 1930, two serials, *Real People* and *The Rise of the Goldbergs*, were being broadcast weekly to a national audience.

Sponsorship of the radio soap opera evolved in much the same way as its programming. Early in the 1930s, advertisers were reluctant to sponsor daytime programs for women. Hence, generous discounts were offered to those advertisers who would purchase an hour of time rather than single

15-minute periods. This system appealed to large advertisers, such as Colgate Palmolive-Peet and Procter and Gamble, offering several brands of products, each of which operated more or less independently but that could trade on the company discount. The hour would be divided among four brands, each of which might proceed to develop its own serial with such success that another hour would soon be added for the same purpose. Because of the preponderance of such advertising, the term "soap opera" was coined. Throughout the three decades that the soaps were on radio, such companies were the primary sponsors, although other products were advertised as well. Serials were sponsored by at least five brands of breakfast cereal, seven brands of toothpaste, a great variety of drug products and home remedies, plus assorted foods, food products, and beverages (Willey, 1961: 100-114).

Advertisers regarded the radio soap operas during their heyday as a great advertising bargain, offered at a cost of as low as 49 cents per thousand listeners. Willey (1961) suggests that it was not so much the lack of sponsorship that killed the radio soap opera, but rather that radio affiliates turned away from network programming. To compete with television, affiliates had to sell their time at the highest possible rate. They could make more money by selling time locally than they could by carrying the offerings of their network.

Of course, as television drew larger audiences, sponsors also became disenchanted with radio. Procter and Gamble, which had been the largest sponsor of radio soap operas, transferred its allegiance from radio to television in the early 1950s. No soap manufacturers sponsored serials during their last sixteen months on radio. Cereals, laxatives, and various health remedies were the most frequent sponsors during the final years (Willey, 1961: 114). Procter and Gamble formed a production company in the early 1950s to produce television soap operas, and today they are still actively involved in their production (see Chapter 4).

THE GROWTH AND DEMISE OF THE RADIO SERIALS

Both the episodic series and the soap opera had their origins in network national radio. As mentioned earlier, the first nationally broadcast drama on a daily basis was *Amos 'n' Andy*. The characters, Amos and Andy, were rustic blacks, although they were played by two white men. The program had been on the radio in Chicago when, in 1929, the NBC radio network began to broadcast it six days a week for fifteen minutes. *Amos 'n' Andy* was a phenomenal success and, as was to become the pattern of network broadcasting, a success was always followed by imitators. Other daily serials were added to the networks' schedules. These were not daytime dramas, although several were later transferred to daytime a few years after their introduction. One of the most famous of these early serials was *Just Plain Bill,* introduced in 1932 for the evening schedule and transferred to daytime in 1933. *Just Plain Bill* remained on the air until 1955. In 1933 there were still some nightly serial programs, while the number of daytime serials grew from two to nine. Most prominent among the new serials were *The Romance of Helen Trent* and *Ma Perkins,* both of which were to remain on radio until 1960, a tenure of 27 years. By 1935, the number of daytime serials had grown to 19. The 1937-38 season was marked by the continuing growth of daytime drama, bringing the total to 38. That season, *The Guiding Light* was introduced (see Chapter 6). During the 1937-38 season, the networks collaborated on a system of duplication. No less than ten serials were repeated at different hours on different networks, often with different products being advertised. For example, *Pepper Young's Family* was carried at different hours of the day on three networks: NBC Red, NBC Blue, and Mutual (Willey, 1961: 99). This practice was largely discontinued after a single season; in 1938-39, only four of the serials were being repeated, and none was heard more than twice.

The year 1940 was regarded as one of the best for daytime serials. Daytime sales on CBS and NBC amounted to an estimated 26.7 million dollars, most of it from serial drama. The total sponsored time for daytime programs other than serials on the four networks was 4.5 hours per week, as compared with 59.5 sponsored hours of serial drama. At the soap opera's peak, 64 serials were broadcast each day, and most were carried by the national networks. Some listeners complained that there was nothing else on the air during the day. In certain areas of the country, where listeners could only receive either NBC or CBS affiliates, the choice of programming was indeed limited. In large cities, listeners had a greater variety of programs from which to choose. Still, the Hooper ratings for daytime drama in 1940 averaged 6.0 (considered high), and the public's favorite soaps attracted audiences at least half again as large. According to Willey (1961: 115, note 4), these ratings are difficult to translate into actual number of listeners with any degree of accuracy. The consensus is that in 1940 about 20 million women (approximately half the women at home during the day) listened to two or more serials daily. (Audience size will be discussed in more detail in Chapter 7.)

After 1940, the number of serials on the air decreased. In 1941 the total had dropped to 33. Although a few new titles were added each year, the schedule showed that more and more listeners were tuning in to the veteran series. Of course, some old serials were dropped, such as *The Goldbergs*, which was canceled in 1946 after 17 years on the air. By 1950, the year the soap opera came to television, the number of soaps had dropped to 27. For the next five years, that number remained fairly steady. None of the popular favorites were discontinued, and only one new program, *Women in My House*, lasted beyond a single season (Stedman, 1959).

By 1955, the radio era of the soap opera was over. The number of serials either stayed the same or diminished each year. The total dropped to sixteen in 1956, ten of which were on CBS and the remainder equally divided between NBC and ABC. In 1959-1960, ABC discontinued all of its soaps, NBC all but *True Story*, and CBS all but seven. At that season's end,

NBC discontinued its only serial, and CBS dropped one more, *The Romance of Helen Trent.*

The 1960-61 season was the soap opera's last on radio. It began with six soap operas returning to CBS. In mid-August of 1960, CBS announced that the last Friday in November would be its serials' final broadcast date. Each program thus had time to conclude its varying plots and to resolve current complications and conflicts. According to Willey (1961: 103), none closed with such finality that the plot could not be resumed on a moment's notice, yet none ever returned.

KEY CREATORS AND PRODUCERS

The Hummerts

Probably more than any other, Frank Hummert was responsible for soap operas. Hummert and his future wife, Anne Achenhurst, who was hired as his assistant in 1930, provided the prototype both for the radio content and the organization of production. They were directly responsible for many of the first soap operas. Hummert had been a copy writer with Lord and Thomas, a large New York advertising agency. In 1927 he left that firm to join Blackett and Sample in Chicago. When Hummert joined the agency, it became Blackett-Sample-Hummert, although he was not a partner and held no stock in the company.

According to Stedman (1977: 255), Frank Hummert was looking for a program formula to suit the housewife listener home during the day. *Stolen Husband,* the first daytime serial produced by the Hummerts in 1931, failed, but through that failure they learned what elements were necessary to make future programs a success, such as slowing the story plots (Stedman, 1977:236). Among the many soap operas they were to produce over the years were: *Our Gal Sunday, Romance of Helen Trent, Backstage Wife, Just Plain Bill, Ma*

Perkins, John's Other Wife, David Harum, and several others (Stedman, 1977: 499-503).

In 1944 the Hummerts split with Blackett and Sample to form Hummert Radio Productions. The Hummerts had become so powerful that they could afford to be independent. Their company became the largest operation of its kind, "a veritable assembly-line of soap operas" (Dunning, 1976: 55). Hummert Radio Productions handled the business and a subsidiary, Air Features, handled production. James Thurber (1948) claims that they employed over 100 writers during the years they were producing soap operas. Air Features employed as many as 16 writers and editors at one time. Anne Hummert created many of the stories by dictating thin plot lines to her secretary, with writers adding the dialogue.

The first soap opera broadcast on national radio was *Betty and Bob,* created, of course, by the Hummerts. The serial lasted seven years, which was not long by soap standards. Its early success paved the way for many serials that were to follow. *Betty and Bob* established the form, the content, and the production style used by the Hummerts.

Betty and Bob had all the ingredients of a successful soap opera. Betty was a stenographer, with whom her boss, Bob Drake, fell in love. Disowned by his millionaire father when he married Betty, Bob was ready for neither marriage nor financial independence. He was attractive to other women, jealous and immature, and unable to hold a job. During the show's seven-year run, the Drakes had a child, were divorced, finally remarried. After two years of "high" ratings, their audience began to decline — a response attributed to the many episodes focusing on their son. In many of the other serials, childless couples were the rule. After *Betty and Bob,* children rarely played major roles in a plot or story line. What children there were lived subterranean lives; they were spoken of only occasionally and rarely heard from. Attitudes about children are part of the soap opera mystique. Good characters like children, bad characters do not, and yet almost no one is shown taking care of children (Goldsen, 1977).

Those familiar with the domestic novel and "confession" short stories will recognize the basic theme of *Betty and Bob*. Ostensibly a love story, it was actually about the problems of marriage in modern society. The story of the secretary who marries her boss is one of the most common themes in women's romantic fiction. One has only to read modern romance novels to know that the story is still popular. (In the current television soap opera, *All My Children*, Dr. Charles Tyler married his secretary, Mona Kane.) As in the confession story, suffering was an underlying theme of *Betty and Bob*. Their marriage was not a happy one. By late 1936, *Betty and Bob* had, as their announcer put it, "surmounted everything, divorce, misunderstanding, the interference of other people and sometimes the worst of all foes, the passage of time." Other topics in *Betty and Bob* would become the mainstay of the soap opera: fidelity, jealousy, divorce, child rearing (or not), family, and romantic love.

The Hummerts contributed more to the structure of soaps than to their modern content. Because of their factory-produced writing company and their conceptions of the housewife audience, the Hummerts were responsible for such basic characteristics as redundancy — characters telling each other what happened the previous day so that listeners will not miss any important plot developments.

Irna Phillips

The other person credited with helping to create the soap opera is Irna Phillips. The Hummerts were essentially producers, although Anne Hummert wrote as well. Irna Phillips was a writer from the beginning, and she remained a writer until she died in 1974. She did not produce her own serials but developed and wrote many different soap operas that were broadcast on radio, as well as several soaps for television. The most important for our purposes is *The Guiding Light*, which was introduced in 1937, discontinued on radio in 1956, and is still broadcast on television. Although the content and characters have changed substantially, it is the longest-running show in broadcasting history (see Chapter 6).

Irna Phillips was a graduate of the University of Illinois and did postgraduate work at the University of Wisconsin. Both she and Anne Hummert occupied a socioeconomic class above their audiences. Phillips started her working career as a schoolteacher fascinated with broadcasting. In 1930 she was hired as an actress by WGN in Chicago and later moved from acting to writing. Phillips is credited with developing the first daytime serial for women, *Painted Dreams*. *Painted Dreams* failed to attract a sponsor, and its original run on WGN was short. Later, the title was used for another soap written by Bess Flynn and Kay Chase.

When discussing the radio soap opera, most analysts distinguish between those created by Irna Phillips and those produced by the Hummerts. One difference was that from the beginning, and continuing on into television, Irna Phillips actually wrote much of her material. According to some reports, she wrote over 2 million words a year. Using a large month-by-month word chart, Phillips plotted and wrote as many as six soaps at once, dictating the action to her secretary. She maintained a lively interest in acting, writing, and directing until the day she died. Finally, while the Hummerts traded on the melodramatic, Phillips did not. The *Guiding Light* served as the prototype for the television soap opera, and Agnes Nixon (1970), the "mother" of so many soap operas still on the air today, worked as an apprentice for Phillips.

All writers were dependent on advertising agencies and production companies. If Phillips had not been supported by advertising dollars, she would never have had the opportunity to display her talents nationally. Indeed, one of the soap operas that Phillips originated was produced by the Hummerts — *The Lonely Women*. Phillips, however, worked in radio mainly for the Compton agency, which, along with other large advertising companies such as Benton and

Bowles and Young and Rubicam, competed with the Hummerts for sponsors' support. As a writer of television soaps, she worked exclusively for Procter and Gamble. In contrast to the Hummerts, Irna Phillips's contributions to the soaps were primarily through the content rather than form or production style. Her concern with the family and traditional views of women's roles and values are still reflected in the soaps produced by Procter and Gamble.

In an interview shortly before her death in 1974, Phillips (Broadcasting, 1972) explained her "soap" philosophy:

> The essence of the drama is still conflict, of course — conflict within each person, conflict between two people. But these relationships don't have to be sordid to be interesting. I'm trying to get back to the fundamentals: for example, the way in which a death in the family, or serious illness, brings members of the family closer together, gives them a real sense of how much they're dependent on each other.

There were other prolific writers in addition to Irna Phillips. Robert Andrews, who worked for the Hummerts, and Elaine Carrington, who developed *Pepper Young's Family* and *When a Girl Marries,* are frequently mentioned by soap opera historians (see Higby, 1968; Stedman, 1977). However, the Hummerts and Irna Phillips are clearly the most important creators — Phillips because she developed the modern soap opera content, and the Hummerts because they developed the production style.

CONCLUSION

From their inception, soap operas more than any other genre, including the evening serials, have reflected the economic and social conditions under which they were and are produced. As in most American fiction, content trends reflect a basic commitment to individualism, but in the soaps individualistic values are interspersed with problems and suffering most likely to be encountered by women. Although generalizations about soap content are difficult to make, in that systematic (or even unsystematic) content analyses of the radio soap operas over time are not available, one generalization can be made. Regardless of their similarity and diversity as to subjects, soap operas are about women and their place in the social world. This topic will be elaborated in Chapters 5 and 6.

National radio bringing "free" entertainment into the home fit the spirit and context into which it was born. The American society of 1982 was born in the 1920s. For example, automobile registration rose from 9.3 million in 1921 to 23.1 million in 1929; telephone ownership rose from 14.3 million in 1922 to 20.3 million by the end of 1930; the domestic use of electricity increased 135 percent in the twenties; and the first scheduled air service was begun in 1926. During that decade the motion picture industry soared; by 1930, it was worth 2 billion dollars, employing 325,000 people, and attracting an audience of up to 15 million a week (Spaulding, 1979).

Of all the innovations of the 1920s, only the automobile was more important than radio. Never as important financially as the movies and possibly other forms of culture, such as the magazine industry, radio was nonetheless by far the most important new mass medium of communications. With the advent of national radio, advertisers, political leaders, and business interests were able to reach the entire nation with the same message simultaneously. Political leaders' strategic use of radio during the 1930s is well documented. Both Roosevelt and Hitler were expert in presenting their views over that medium. Not recognized was radio's power in establishing what is called by some the "consumer society." Because radio became a commercial rather than a public medium, it was instrumental as a mechanism of social control and social integration in American society. By 1930, 50 percent of all households in the United States had radios, and by 1940, 98 percent of U.S. households contained one or more. The story of the Orson Welles program, *War of the Worlds,* is usually recounted to show radio's ability to incite people to action (Cantril, 1940; Koch, 1970). This event, which caused listeners to leave their homes and seek shelter because they believed that there was an invasion from outer space, actually was unique. The power of radio was subtle and pervasive. Radio transmitted the Anglo-American culture of the nineteenth and twentieth centuries to all elements of the society, along with commercial advertisements. Through radio, the culture was both transformed and perpetuated. In addition, radio's programming format was transferred almost intact to television. Radio provided television's basic structure for all time periods. There is little doubt that the radio industry, which established program types, time limitations, and the commercial break, provided the context for television as we know it today.

Throughout the remainder of the book, we will compare the television soap opera to the radio soap opera when appropriate. Although prime-time drama now represents a marriage between movie and radio formats (Cantor, 1982; FCC, 1980), the soap opera remains close in form and production style to its predecessors on radio. In the following chapter, which discusses the transfer of the soaps to television and their present production process, the modern soap opera's debt to radio will be further specified.

NOTES

1. For a general discussion of the rise of broadcasting in the United States, see Barnouw (1966, 1968). Fred MacDonald's *Don't Touch That Dial* (1979) is highly recommended, especially for its chapter on the soap opera. Also see Stedman (1977) for a complete history of serial drama, including movies, prime-time and daytime.

2. In 1943 the Supreme Court ordered NBC to divest itself of its Blue network (owning two networks was considered a monopoly), and NBC Blue became ABC under different ownership (see MacDonald, 1979: 76).

4

SOAPS ON TELEVISION

The differences between soap opera production and that of prime-time television. Considers the power and control that creative people have over content. Describes the actual production of a soap opera.

When the last soap opera left radio in 1960, daytime serials were already an established form of television programming. Despite enthusiasm about television's potential, some experts were at first doubtful that television could carry serial drama successfully, especially in the daytime. Charles Siepmann (1950: 345) argued that television serials would overwhelm the daytime audience of women occupied with household duties. He wrote:

> Television, which claims the attention of both eye and ear, is likely to prove altogether too exacting in its demands for daytime audiences. Women will probably continue to listen to serial drama and other daytime radio features.

Siepmann believed that television's demands on attention and the "strain" involved in using both eyes and ears over prolonged periods of time were being underestimated. Although he and others predicted that television serials would not succeed, they eventually became television's most profitable programs.

PRODUCTION AND CONTROL

According to *TV Guide* (1956), the first regular serial program on television was *A Woman To Remember,* introduced in 1947 as a sustaining program of the now defunct Dumont Television Network. The article does not indicate whether it was a daytime or prime-time serial. Its life was short because it did not attract advertiser support. In December 1950, Procter and Gamble introduced and sponsored *The First Hundred Years* on CBS, a program describing the problems of newlyweds. *The First Hundred Years* was followed by *Miss Susan* (a Woman Alone story) and *Hawkins Falls* (a Family Saga) on NBC. CBS introduced three more soap operas in 1951: *The Egg and I,* based on Betty McDonald's humorous novel; *Search for Tomorrow,* still on the air in 1982; and *Love of Life,* which ran continuously until 1980. ABC did not support serial drama during the daytime until later in the decade, but by the end of 1950 all three television networks had established soap operas as part of their regular daytime schedule.

Since the 1950s, daytime and prime-time television have been different. For example, the evening dramatic shows on the air during the early 1950s were considered excellent by critics, who compared them to the best theater productions. Because of these productions, the first few years after World War II are known as the "Golden Years of Television." In contrast, soap operas were never critical successes and were often maligned as low level, in production quality as well as in content. The soaps were considered "radio with pictures." However, there was one similarity between the two types of drama: Both were controlled by the sponsors and produced by advertising agencies.

Theater drama has virtually disappeared from the airways, supplanted by filmed drama (Barnouw, 1975; Cantor, 1980). In contrast, soap operas have flourished. Until 1983 there was a steady increase in the time the networks alloted to their broadcast. In 1960, soap operas were on the air 210 minutes each broadcast day (Katzman, 1972). In 1970, they were on 510 minutes, in 1982, 690 minutes, and in 1983, 600 minutes. The actual number of individual programs has also decreased: 17 in 1970-71, 14 in 1982, and 12 in 1983. Some soaps in the 1950s lasted only 15 minutes. By the end of the 1960s all were 30 minutes, and in 1982 nine were one hour and the others one-half hour long.

The advertisers still produce soap operas, along with ABC, which in the late 1960s and early 1970s invested heavily in their production, and one independent production company (Corday, with Columbia Pictures TV). Procter and Gamble produces six soaps. (They also produced *Texas* until it was dropped from the schedule on December 31, 1982 along with *The Doctors*, produced by Colgate-Palmolive). Now that *The Doctors* has been canceled, Colgate-Palmolive will no longer be involved in producing. Three soaps are produced either wholly or partially by Columbia Pictures TV. Its entry into the production of daytime television is relatively recent. The remaining four shows are produced by ABC. Although all soap operas are produced in broadcast studios, ABC is the only network that produces its own soap operas directly. Table 4.1 shows each show on the air in 1982, the date it was introduced, the network broadcasting it, and the company producing it.

As shown in the table, eight soap operas were introduced in 1965 or before, and six since 1968. Three of the six newer soaps are on ABC and, along with *General Hospital,* they have enjoyed the highest ratings in the last five years. *General Hospital* can also be considered a new program, because in 1977 it was changed from an old-fashioned show to one that is young and trendy (Newsweek, 1981). A soap opera can be on the air for years and not necessarily be static in its production and content. As we will show in the audience chapter, besides having the highest ratings, ABC has also managed to capture more young viewers than the other two networks combined. While there is not a lot of research on these shows' individual characteristics, it seems from journalistic accounts that the highly rated ABC shows, especially

TABLE 4.1   Soap Operas on the Air in 1982

Date Introduced	Network	Name	Production Company
1951	NBC*	Search for Tomorrow	Procter and Gamble
1952	CBS	Guiding Light	Procter and Gamble
1956	CBS	As the World Turns	Procter and Gamble
1956	ABC*	Edge of Night	Procter and Gamble
1963	ABC	General Hospital	ABC
1963	NBC**	The Doctors	Colgate-Palmolive
1965	NBC	Days of Our Lives	Corday (with Columbia)
1968	ABC	One Life to Live	ABC
1970	ABC	All My Children	ABC
1973	CBS	The Young and the Restless	Columbia Pictures
1975	ABC	Ryan's Hope	ABC
1980	NBC**	Texas	Procter and Gamble
1982	CBS	Capitol	Corday (with Columbia)

*Introduced on CBS
**Canceled as of December 31, 1982

General Hospital and *All My Children,* are presenting a more trendy and relevant message to younger viewers.

Prime Time/Daytime

Soap operas came to television as radio with pictures, and to this day, as a genre they are closer to being a broadcasting medium than a film medium. Prime-time serials and series are combinations of film and broadcasting, with some kinds of programs more like soap operas than others. For example, situation comedies resemble soap operas in the kinds of sets used, while the serials on prime time, which are filmed rather than taped, resemble soap operas because they are serials. Overall, the prime-time dramas represent a marriage between the film industry and broadcasting (Cantor, 1982). From the beginning, the soap opera was a broadcasting medium, and it remains so to this day. The distinction between prime-time and daytime drama is a very important one. The soap opera transferred to television a means of production that is unique in dramatic programs. When appropriate, the production process for the soap opera will be described and compared to that of prime-time drama. The emphasis, of course, will be on the soap opera. Prime-time television was covered in detail in an earlier volume for this series (Cantor, 1980).

Both prime-time and daytime programs are usually produced in either Hollywood (Los Angeles, California) or New York by program suppliers or the networks themselves. The first important difference between the two is that the networks are more likely to be directly involved in the production of soap operas, whereas most prime-time television is produced by program suppliers who are independent (in name, at least) of the networks. Another important difference is that all soap operas are taped daily in broadcasting studios, whereas many of the prime-time series are either filmed on location or in studios owned and operated by the major film companies. A series, whether it is filmed or taped, is most often produced in Hollywood. Most soap operas are taped in network-owned stations in New York City. Even those produced in Hollywood are made at broadcasting studios rather than at film studios. *Days of Our Lives* is produced at NBC in Burbank, while *The Young and the Restless* and *Capitol* are made at CBS, and *General Hospital* at the ABC studios, both in Los Angeles.

Who controls prime-time television remains unknown, although several have investigated the problem. Some believe that network control explains prime-time content (Goldsen, 1977; Cantor, 1980). Others see the producers and program suppliers in Hollywood as more powerful (Newcomb and Alley, 1982; Stein, 1979). Although the networks remain powerful, they are clearly dependent on the creative people in Hollywood for the ideas and the films and tapes necessary to fill the three nightly hours known as prime time. The power of the networks over the daytime schedule is far less problematic. Because daytime programs originated in radio and have remained in the hands of network executives, almost exclusively in New York, the power to decide content and schedule is rarely debated.

Three important characteristics distinguish the production process of daytime series from those seen during prime time. The most obvious difference is that daytime series are shown daily (five days a week). By contrast, one episode per week is the overwhelming norm for prime-time series. A daytime series exhibits as many as 260 original episodes in a year (52 weeks, five episodes per week), and rarely fewer than 240. With a prime-time series, 22 original episodes are usually produced each year. Second, although daytime contracts are written for short periods of time, usually three months, they are more likely to be renewed than those written for prime time. Once a soap opera is on the air, it is likely to stay on for some time. Most new prime-time series are unlikely to finish more than one season. Third, the networks normally pay directly for most or all of the "below-the-line" costs of a daytime series that are licensed to others. Of course, when they own the series, they pay all the costs. Below-the-line costs are those incurred in the technical production of the program, such as cameras, tape facilities, and supporting personnel. For prime-time series, the networks normally pay a fixed license fee for each episode, and the producer pays the below-the-line costs out of that fee. A prime-time contract, however, also usually contains a "union protection date," which provides for an increase in the license fee by an amount sufficient to cover any union wage increases that occur after the date the contract was issued.

There is little overlap between the suppliers of original daytime programming and those of prime-time programming (FCC, 1980). Prime-time producers do not supply original programs for daytime television. Their participation in daytime programming is limited to reruns of prime-time series. Few independent producers have been involved in providing soap operas, either. Rather, advertisers and networks have had virtually exclusive control over the soaps. Just as prime-time producers rarely go into the daytime market, since the early 1960s soap opera producers almost never go into the prime-time market. One exception, Procter and

Gamble, is still very actively involved in daytime production and has occasionally gone into the prime-time market as well. In 1978 it co-produced the short-lived comedy series, *Shirley,* and was responsible for the mini-series, *Marco Polo.* The reasons that more advertisers are not directly involved in the production of prime-time series have been discussed in detail elsewhere (see Barnouw, 1975; Cantor, 1980). The primary reason is the quiz scandals and the congressional probes resulting from the scandals in 1959. These events caused the networks to reorganize their production methods and remove the advertisers from direct involvement in prime-time production. Other factors also contributed to the advertisers' removal from the prime-time market. Since 1959, dramatic series costs have risen substantially. At the same time, prime-time series have a very high mortality rate. Also, there is greater sophistication about demographic characteristics and how audiences use television. It is thus more beneficial to both the networks and advertisers to use a "magazine" concept of sponsorship, so that no single advertiser needs to bear the entire cost of production.

The costs of producing daytime serials have also risen significantly over the last two decades. Nevertheless, as will be elaborated below, these programs have remained far less expensive than the typical prime-time series. At one time, the advertisers who produced a soap opera sponsored the entire show. Now, because of the costs, the programs they produce are not necessarily fully sponsored by them. Instead, the advertiser-supplier sponsors a portion and the network sells the remaining time, as it does with other programs.

As noted earlier, daytime serials are canceled far less frequently than prime-time series. Network executives believe that viewers become very attached to a daytime schedule and may order their daily nonviewing activities around the program. For this reason, the networks remain reluctant to subject the daytime schedule to the same juggling that has recently typified prime-time television. Further, the networks believe that it is usually some time before a serial finally builds up its audience. One network executive mentioned in an FCC report (1980: 104) that a show may require three or four years to acquire its audience. Prime-time shows that do not attract large audiences (or the "correct" audience, demographically) are not given a chance to finish the season.

Once a daytime series has established itself in the schedule, it usually remains a long time. As we have emphasized, *The Guiding Light* has been broadcast since 1937, first on radio and later (starting in 1952) on television; *Search for Tomorrow* has been on television since 1951. There are no shows currently on prime-time network television that were originally broadcast on radio, although several popular series such as *Gunsmoke* and *Dragnet* did originate on radio and enjoyed long television runs. *Dragnet* had two separate television runs, one from 1951 to 1959 in black and white, and the second in color from 1967 to 1970. Also, there are no series on television (except reruns) that were on the air before 1970. M*A*S*H, the longest-running television series, was first broadcast in 1972. *All in the Family* was also first broadcast that year, and a spinoff called *Archie's Place*, starring Carroll O'Connor (as did *All in the Family)*, was still on the air in 1982. However, the two shows are different enough in many ways to be considered separate programs. Indeed, all of these programs are exceptions. Presently, to remain on the air during prime time, a series must rank high in the ratings from its inception. Only in exceptional circumstances would a prime-time series be allowed the luxury of building an audience.

During the 1981-1982 season there were approximately 45 evening series on the air and just 14 soap operas. That fact could lead one to surmise that the prime-time series is the more favored of the two forms. However, because the soap operas generate steady profits (as a result of their continuous showings), they are far more valuable to the networks than the prime-time series. Soap operas are the most profitable daytime shows on the air, although the most expensive to produce when compared to game shows, talk shows, and series reruns.

A 30-second commercial during the daytime costs between $5,000 *(The Doctors)* and $27,800 *(General Hospital)*. Thus, the average commercial costs about $16,000 dollars, compared to $75,000 during prime time. These figures would lead one to believe that prime time is the more profitable. More of the daytime revenue is clear profit, however, because daytime programming is so much cheaper to produce. A half-hour prime-time show can cost $350,000. For the same money (or less), a full week of hour-long soap episodes can be produced. Soap operas are particularly profitable for ABC because it owns and produces four out of five of its soaps and because they have had consistently high ratings during the last half of the 1970s. The other networks have licensed some of their soap operas to Procter and Gamble under agreements that give the advertiser favorable rates. This arrangement limits the revenues that CBS and NBC can get from daytime television.

Logically, one might expect a prime-time series to be produced more cheaply than a soap opera because there are so few episodes and because the casts for the series are smaller when compared to those in soap operas. Most series have casts of 10 or fewer on a regular basis, while the cast for a soap is very large; no soap opera on the air has fewer than 25 regular characters. Interestingly, the radio soap opera and radio evening series were similar in both cost and production style. Although prime-time television costs were higher than daytime costs from the beginning, the two diverged dramatically when prime-time production moved from New York to Hollywood in the early fifties and the series began to be filmed rather than produced live.

When the evening programs transferred to film, a star system developed. While the star system in television never became as pronounced as it was in the heyday of Hollywood movies during the 1930s and 1940s, most evening series (even those resembling the soaps in form, such as *Dallas)* trade on the star character(s) for story focus. Hence, actors are closely associated with individual series. By comparison, the large number of characters in a soap opera and the intertwining, continuous plots give more power to the story than the actors. Although actors working in the soaps are well paid and unionized (members of the American Federation of Television and Radio Actors), no soap opera actor commands the kind of salary negotiated by stars of the prime-time shows. Salaries for the other soap opera workers are also lower. Directors, producers, and especially the cadre of writers who simply produce dialogue are relatively low paid in comparison to their counterparts working on a series. Only the chief writer of a soap opera, who can be compared to the on-line producer for a series, is paid wages at all equivalent to those of prime-time creative people. In fact chief soap writers are among the highest paid people working in television. Their salaries, however, do not add substantially to the cost of production, considering the work demanded from them. If their salaries are divided according to the number of scripts they produce, each daily script is far less expensive than a prime-time script for the equivalent length of program.

The sets of a soap opera also help to keep production costs down. Because most of the scenes take place indoors, in a living room, hospital, or office, few sets are needed. Also, the sets can be used, with minor variations, year after year, day after day. Although situation comedies, especially those that are taped in broadcast studios in a fashion similar to the daily soap operas, also need only a few inexpensive sets, the adventure series are often very expensive to produce. In the last few years, more soap opera production has taken place on location, but these events, such as car accidents or an entire sequence out of the country, are still unusual. Some soap operas have more resources than others, especially those produced by ABC, and resources are clearly related to revenue. Overall, however, the cheap sets and the relatively low salaries for actors and other production personnel keep soap opera costs down, while the advertising revenue generated by soap operas guarantees a healthy profit for the networks and suppliers. Should a soap opera be syndicated (rare, but it does happen), it generates additional profit as well. For example, *Dark Shadows* (1961-1968) is no longer being produced but is being syndicated in various markets.

PRODUCING SOAP OPERAS

Creating Soaps

The characteristics of the production process essentially limit the freedom and creativity of almost all participants except the head writer, network officials, and to a lesser degree the executive producer. The overall production organization includes many positions, all of which play some role in the production process. Film-making and broadcasting production are organized essentially hierarchically, although the production is craftlike. This means that individuals are "professionalized" for specific tasks, either through professional training or apprenticeship on the job.

Soap opera production is still similar to the system that the Hummerts developed in the days of radio. However, because any medium which includes both visual and audio components is far more complicated than production without the visual, more people are needed and the process is more time-consuming. Eighty people are needed to produce five daily episodes of *The Guiding Light,* including actors and writers (Intintoli, n.d.). The supervising producer, the executive producer, and the head writer are most responsible for shaping the content of the Procter and Gamble soaps. A distinct difference between those soap operas produced by the latter and those produced by the networks is that the networks essentially ignore the Procter and Gamble shows as far as daily operations and direction are concerned; that is, the company is in complete control (LeMay, 1981). When the networks act as executive producers through their representatives, there is a great deal of network interference. Procter and Gamble is organized so that the supervising producer is in charge of several soap operas. The same producer was responsible for *Search for Tomorrow, The Guiding Light,* and *The Edge of Night.* Essentially, the supervising producer is a business executive rather than a creator. He or she is in charge of budget and major personnel decisions, but because of the nature of production, an executive producer is also involved with story development and casting. It is the executive producer who works closely with the daily production process. The executive producer is directly under the head writer on a daily basis, particularly in terms of making script changes or cuts, and supervises the on-line producers and production staff. The involvement of the executive producer in the actual taping and rehearsals can vary. Intintoli (n.d.) says that the executive producers were rarely involved in the decisions for those shows where he observed production *(Search for Tomorrow* and *Guiding Light).* In network shows, especially the ABC-produced shows, the executive producer was far more actively involved. There is no question that the producer has a great deal of power in all television production, but in daytime production he or she is subordinate to the head writer in the decision-making process concerning content.

It is generally recognized that prime-time television is a producer's medium, and that soap operas are a writer's medium. In soap operas, story is very important. Producers believe that what sells the viewer is not the actors nor the production quality, but rather the plots and characters. All sources report that the head writer has the power, within the limits of the genre, to determine content. Of course, when writers no longer please the network executives or the production company, they can be replaced, but even then scripts are not changed in the same way by producers as they are in prime time.

Early in the history of the soap opera, a writing style was established that was unique to the medium. Because soaps are aired every day, the need for so many scripts or programs each year led early on to a division of labor among writers. Anne Hummert, for example, developed stories and plots but left the dialogue-writing to others. Probably no other person wrote as many soap opera episodes as Irna Phillips, but even she was forced to hire others to help her when the soap opera expanded from 15 to 30 minutes.

The demands of writing for 30 and 60 minutes of programming has led to a pattern followed by all programs, whether network- or advertiser-produced. There is a head writer, who is important and powerful, and a number of subwriters or "dialoguers." The dialogue writers are usually contracted by the head writer and are responsible for writing the actual script. The head writer develops the various plots and stories, as well as the characters. (New characters are added and old ones dropped with regularity on the soaps.) Head writers change, but the head writer must be familiar with past, present, and future stories. The plots are very complicated on one level, especially keeping track of various characters. There are examples of characters, presumed dead, who come back to life, and of characters who frequently marry and divorce the same or different people. Writers must keep track of the characters' biographies, especially of the basic family members in a cast. In the last five years, *General Hospital* has had at least three head writers. *Days of Our Lives* has had more than three. Each of these writers (or writing teams) has had to become familiar with the history of the show. In contrast, William Bell continues to create *The Young and the Restless* as he has from its inception in 1973.

Ultimately, however, the head writer is hired by the production company or the network and must satisfy its conditions. This is part of the structure and culture of all television production, whether for prime time or daytime. Ratings, which will be discussed in Chapter 7, are important for daytime, although not as important as for nighttime. Intintoli (n.d.) suggests that if a show is doing poorly, the writer may have greater freedom to innovate, but writers may also be replaced when the ratings are low. The head writer's position is one of power but, as with all creators for television, it is also precarious. Everyone involved in the production process is limited by the constraints of ratings, corporate policy, budget, cast, technical and logistical capability, and the implications of the past story, character, and "style" of a show.

The positions of dialogue writers and others on the production team are almost without power or freedom. Such roles by definition, are powerless. Duties entail supplying appropriate dialogue and minor incidents. The head writer supplies the outlines for the stories, and even when the stories are very brief, he or she will edit the scripts, often revising them extensively.

On the Sets

Soap operas continued to be broadcast live throughout the 1960s, when virtually all prime-time programs were being filmed. *As the World Turns* and *The Edge of Night* were produced almost entirely live until the mid-1970s, when some shows went from a half-hour to an hour. *As the World Turns* stayed live so long because it was the creation of Irna Phillips. She and Procter and Gamble preferred their soap operas to be broadcast live. Phillips believed that taping a show took the excitement out of the production. With live production, of course, there are no retakes. The actors know they have to do it right the first time.

Although all shows are now video-taped, with occasional use of stock film shots, because a show a day must be produced, the producers and directors operate similarly in style to the way they did when the shows were produced live. A comparison of how *As the World Turns* was produced in 1974 with the production of *Days of Our Lives* in 1982 will show how the tasks remain similar, even though *Days of Our Lives* is taped. *Days of Our Lives* was chosen over a more popular show because its budget is limited. The more popular shows, such as *General Hospital, All My Children,* and *The Young and the Restless,* have more resources and as resources increase, the production style becomes closer to film production. For example, more episodes are taped "on location" rather than in studios than in the past. However, there is an organization of production that has developed for all soap operas regardless of their profits, ratings, or resources.

Live Production

The day at *As the World Turns* started early in 1974. The director and the players began at 7:30 a.m., reading lines and walking through each scene. While the actors worked out their exchanges, the production assistant timed every moment with a stopwatch. Each scene had to be timed down to the last second. Dialogue fill-ins or changes were made on the spot. When the walk-through was completed, the director made decisions about the camera shots. *As the World Turns* used three, and sometimes four cameras.

In the middle of the morning, a first-on camera rehearsal was held. The director, working from the control booth, called out the numbers indicating the camera shot he wanted. Dress rehearsal began about an hour before showtime. There were no stops and starts. When mistakes were made, they were noted by the production people and everything kept going. Even the commercials were run. The show was aired at 2:30 p.m. daily. By 1974, music and voice-overs were being audio-taped a day or so earlier, and some scenes were video-taped or filmed and inserted later. For example, a fire scene or other action scenes could not be done live. The point here is that is is possible to do a live broadcast of a play each day for close to 20 years, as occurred on network television (see Ward, 1974, for a full description).

Taping an Episode

By 1975, all shows were being video-taped. Video-taping became a necessity when the shows went from one-half hour to an hour in length. The advantages of video-taping are obvious. Networks and affiliates have more flexibility with schedules, and of course some editing and retakes are possible.

Yet because so many episodes are needed each week, video-taping is not all that different from live production. The day at *Days of Our Lives* in 1982 was very similar to the one described above. The cast assembled at 8:00 in the morning. Players read their lines and walked through each scene. An hour script is approximately 70 pages long, and before the day ended, all 70 pages were video-taped. People who understand the complexity of television production consider that a miraculous feat.

The crew starts at 6:00 a.m., blocking out scenes and deciding on camera shots. The actors do not go through what is called a camera block until 8:30. This is a run-through of the script where the director and producer work with the actors and the script to be sure that all moves, actions, and dialogue are congruent with each other. For example, one character must not stand in front of another who is speaking lines. If there is a barroom scene, a waiter must move behind the main characters so that they are not blocked from the view of the camera.

After lunch there is a dress rehearsal, followed by a half-hour break for "notes," at which point the director and producer inform the actors where there are problems. A dress rehearsal is needed so that each scene can be timed and perfected before taping. On each camera there is a sheet listing the shots that camera will take and the sequence the camera person must follow. Because *Days of Our Lives* is a relatively low-cost production, most of the time only two cameras are used. The rehearsal starts around 12:45 p.m. and lasts until about 2:00 in the afternoon.

The actual taping can take anywhere from two hours and 15 minutes (the ideal) to three hours or more. Usually the day is done by 5:00 p.m., but if there are problems it can last longer. There are approximately ten or twelve scenes that take place on six sets. Most scenes were taped only once, as though the production were live, but several times the actors, even with the help of cue cards, did not deliver the lines satisfactorily. Whether lines were missed or whether the producer did not like the way a scene was played, the scene was reshot.

A taped show will be edited and shown two weeks after the taping. Taping a show allows the director and producer more freedom to make last-minute changes, compared with a live show. All scenes that take place on a particular set, whether or not they follow in sequence, are taped at the same time. However, because of the way a soap opera is written, that luxury is rare. In the episodes we observed there were ten scenes, and only four took place on the same set. Often, inserts from other programs will be used. Although taping allows some of the techniques common in filming to be adopted, the limited time available means that it is not possible to reshoot too frequently.

The studio where *Days of Our Lives* is shot is a barnlike room (as are most studios) large enough to accommodate the six sets and still have room to move the camera and crew around the area easily. Each scene ran for approximately seven or eight minutes. Commercials are added in at the editing stage.

The production process is similar for all soap operas, while that for prime-time drama varies according to studio policy and program category. Situation comedies are videotaped, often in front of a live audience. However, the rehearsal time, rather than being a few hours long, is several days. A filmed, one-hour prime-time show takes eight days to shoot, a half-hour program four or five days. Our observations at both prime-time filming and that of *Days of Our Lives* are corroborated by others. Soap opera production, regardless of who owns the show and where it is produced (New York or Los Angeles) is almost always uniform. Differences in the quality of shows appear because of the amount of money available to each company. Because each show must be broadcast so soon (one or two weeks) after it is produced, and because so many episodes are needed, the soap opera remains close to its predecessor on radio.

Working on Soaps

Soap operas, like all broadcasting and film media, are produced collectively. The content of each medium or genre varies, not so much because of who has the power, but rather because power becomes concentrated in certain roles as a result of the nature of the shows themselves. Prime-time episodic series are a producer's medium. The reasons for this have been debated (see Cantor, 1980; Newcomb and Alley, 1982; Stein, 1979), but all agree that the producer is more powerful than the writer or director. In contrast, the theatrical film is a director's medium, since a film is commonly associated with its director or director-writer.

The soap opera is a writer's medium. The chief writer essentially controls the content. Although production is important and all television is produced by a team, production qualities are not as important in soap operas as they are in prime-time drama. In the soap opera, stories and characters are most important.

In all soap operas, there is little variation from the written script. There is simply no time to make major changes, given the soaps' tight production schedules. In addition, the writers are often quite a long distance from the production. For example, *The Young and the Restless* is shot in Hollywood but written in Chicago. If a scene runs too long, unnecessary lines may be cut, but meaning is rarely changed. Occasionally, an actor who has played a character for a long period of time will inform the producer that a portrayal is "out of character," and the writer will be so informed. Mostly, though, the writer's word is law. Changes in script, if any, are minor. In one script from *Days of Our Lives,* a character had a line informing the audience that she had bought a king-size bed. In the taping, the line was changed and the audience was told only that she had bought a bed. The reason for the change was that the prop department had no king-size beds.

Writing for the Soaps

Harding LeMay (1981), who was hired by Irna Phillips and wrote *Another World* for eight years, explains that writing a soap opera is like writing three full-length plays simultaneously: When one reaches the end of the final act of the first play, one is well into the second act of another and the beginning of a third. The soap opera, according to LeMay, has no beginning or end. It is one endless middle.

The following analogy is attributed to writer William Bell *(The Young and the Restless):* Each story can be compared to a roll of paper towels. Three of four rolls are lined up on a wall, and each has a different length of paper pulled from it, representing an ongoing story at a given stage of development.

This quality of the soap opera (and here they are all the same) means that someone has to have a firm grip on the stories and the characters. Each soap opera has at least 25 or 30 who are involved in one or more of the continuing stories. The chief writer thus becomes the most powerful person in determining content, in contrast to other forms of film and television production where the writer is subordinate to the producer or director. Scripts, as previously noted, are not often changed, and the final taping reflects what the writer had in mind. For soap operas, there is a division of labor among the chief writer and the subwriters and dialoguers, but the head writer controls the process.

This process is very different from the process of writing a movie or an episodic series segment. For episodic series, free-lance writers are often used. Even when writers are hired on a constractual basis for a particular show, they often have their scripts changed by the producer or by a committee consisting of the producer, other writers, and the director (at a story conference). The soap opera writer is often the only person familiar with the past, present, and future of a story. Each year or so, the "bible" is written, projecting the stories and adding new ones (that is, taking down all of the paper rolls and adding a new one). The bible is written by the head writer. In addition, he or she outlines each episode.

Some soap opera writers, because of their creative power, have become associated with their creations. Irna Phillips is probably the most renowned and, as has been elaborated throughout, her influence and power were enormous. In addition to creating many soap operas, she provided an internship for other writers who worked for her. Agnes Nixon (1970), the originator of *All My Children* and *One Life to Live* for ABC, is the best-known living soap writer. Nixon worked as a dialoguer under Phillips in order to learn her craft and eventually became the head writer on *Guiding Light* and co-creator (with Phillips) of *As the World Turns*. Harding LeMay (1981), head writer for *Another World* for eight years, also worked directly for Phillips.

Acting on the Soaps

Soap operas provide work for about 500 actors a year, mostly in New York, but also in Los Angeles. Actors on daytime television are not as powerful as those who become stars on prime time, since prime-time series are usually built around one or two major characters. Without including spinoffs, it is rare to have even a supporting actor leave a prime-time series, except by natural death. Occasionally actors are "written out" of an evening series, but such events are as unusual on prime time as they are common on daytime.

Of course, there are stars and supporting actors who do leave, either because they tire of roles, are dissatisfied with salary arrangements, or have other grievances. Examples are Martin Landau and Barbara Baine *(Mission Impossible)*, Farrah Fawcett-Majors *(Charlie's Angels)*, and MacLean Stevenson (M*A*S*H). We might note, however, that all of these had other major co-stars on their respective shows. In cases where a single star is identified with a series, that person becomes irreplaceable. Thus, when Freddie Prinze (who played Chico on *Chico and the Man)* committed suicide, the show went off the air. Likewise, when Mary Tyler Moore tired of her role, *The Mary Tyler Moore Show* had to be dropped.

While the star system has not been a major consideration in casting parts on soap operas, there are a number of players who have stayed in the same role for so many years that they are associated with their respective parts. Others have used soaps as training for prime-time, film, and commercial work. Of these, perhaps the best-known are Jill Clayburgh and Marsha Mason.

Compared to other acting jobs, acting in soap operas is considered trivial, even by actors themselves. Intintoli (n.d.) noted that actors on the sets he observed made fun of their lines. We also observed a certain amount of cynicism. At the same time, we were impressed by the effort some actors gave to their parts. Several of the older actors on *Days of Our Lives* commented that because the characters were so consistent, rehearsal time was not as necessary as it might be in a single-episode production. Each day's shooting was a rehearsal for the next. The serious actors on soaps often ask for time off to play summer stock and travelling productions, and to be able to play more creative roles than those offered on soap operas. For younger actors, the exposure and training are not available elsewhere.

CONCLUSION

The production and economics of daytime serials and prime-time drama are very different, so different that each can be considered a separate type of broadcasting. The soap opera remains a broadcasting medium, as it was from the beginning. Prime-time television production cannot be distinguished from film production. As cable television becomes more commonplace, the line between film and television production will become more and more blurred.

Elsewhere, Cantor (1980) has suggested that the content of prime-time drama is not a reflection of the tastes and ideology of its creators, nor of those who control the channels of communication; rather, it represents a negotiated struggle between those who value the content for commercial purposes and those who value it for cultural, social, or artistic reasons. One reason the soap opera has flourished is that it has not been the object of as much controversy. More important, however, soap operas continue to enjoy popularity with the networks because of the advertising revenue they generate, and because the investment required is comparatively low. Even the size of the audience required for success and profit is more limited than for prime time. Thus, a serial can afford the luxury of building an audience, whereas a prime-time series cannot. Although there have been changes in production which are related to technological advances, the soaps remain remarkably similar to their predecessors on radio. In the following chapters, we consider how much the audience and content have changed in the last fifty years. The future of the soap opera in America will also be considered. From this analysis, it is clear that their past, present, and future are tied to the fate of commercial broadcasting and to the role advertisers play in providing entertainment for viewers.

5

SOAP OPERA CONTENT

Discusses in depth the soaps' portrayal of female culture, showing how sex, social issues and problems, illness and health are presented to viewers. Also examines "dramatic demography," social status, and sex role inequalities. Radio soap operas are compared to television.

In *The Official Soap Opera Annual,* editor Bayna Laub (1977) states that soap operas, "in their faithful portrayal of all the happiness and the sadness, the triumphs and the tragedies, the successes and the failures in their characters' lives — prove once more that today's soap operas are indeed a reflection of life." That statement is only one example of many found in the popular literature, suggesting that modern soap operas, those from approximately 1970 on, are more realistic than the "moralistic fifteen-minute radio melodramas," their predecessors (Laub, 1977). We contend that no genre is "realistic." Rather, through stories, a fictionalized representation of our social structure and social relations are presented. These fictionalized representations provide a mirror of the world, showing how power is allocated in society and how dominance and submission are idealized (Gerbner, 1972). The social demography of the soaps, their locales, and in particular the way social status, love and romance, sickness and health, crime and violence are presented are at best a stylized representation of the real world and, at worst, reflect the continuing inequalities and disparities between races, classes, and the sexes in American society.

It is generally accepted that the modern soap opera is more realistic than some radio soaps, especially those produced by the Hummerts (Stedman, 1977), which were considered melodramatic, and most anes, soap opera time is "real time" rather than "film" time, except that events of a few hours' duration can be extended into a two-week broadcast period. In comparison, in prime-time drama the expanse of years may be compressed into two hours. Horace Newcomb (1974: 161) subtitles his chapter on the soap opera, "Approaching the Real World." Newcomb claims that soap opera audiences and prime-time audiences are each presented with a different set of problems. Soap opera problems are more closely related to those that the audience also experiences. Although these problems may be more "real," they are not reality. Because they are targeted to women, soap operas present a different fictional world from that of prime time. Part of our purpose here is to show how soap operas create and re-create the social world day after day, and to show how these creations are genre-specific.

This chapter is divided into two parts. In both, radio soap operas will be compared to their successors on television, and daytime series will be compared to prime-time series. Here we focus on changes and differences in content, not form, which has been discussed earlier in the book. Of course, not all content will be discussed. Rather, we shall examine three major characteristics of television drama. The first section focuses on the locale of the stories and the way sex and moral issues are presented. Later, we examine how sex roles and social status have changed in the soaps over time and compare the social demography of the prime-time series to that found on the soaps. In addition, issues relating to equality between the sexes, such as who dominates conversations and who works at what occupations, will be discussed.

Before we begin the analysis, a few words about methodology. Various investigators use different research techniques and theoretical perspectives to analyze media content. The most commonly used method is content analysis (Holsti, 1969; Krippendorf, 1982). Because the researcher using this method counts what is on the air, what is not shown is rarely discussed. However, it is not the method that make the available analyses difficult to use for our purposes, but rather the *emphases* in these analyses. There is no reason, for example, that we should not be able to discuss with more authority what happened to the Woman Alone, a favorite radio theme that seems to have disappeared from the television soap opera. Judging from the way recent social science research has been carried out, however, this theme has simply not seemed important to researchers.

Another criticism is in order here. There are differences among the soap operas themselves, as has been suggested in Chapter 4. By counting sexual acts or violence in all programs presented in a certain time period, the differences among the individual programs are not highlighted, while the similarities are. Others have criticized content analysis from several perspectives. One of the most common criticisms comes from those who believe that an analysis of content should incorporate some interpretation of meaning, since themes and myths become lost when content is divided into specific categories.[1] Nevertheless, what we do know about the soap opera comes mostly from such content analyses, carried out by social scientists whose care and rigor are not being disputed. Along with findings from content analyses, journalistic accounts and literary critiques will also be incorporated when appropriate.

For our analysis of the radio soap opera, we are drawing on three sources: Raymond Stedman (1959, 1977); Rudolf

Arnheim (1944), who did the only reasonably rigorous, systematic content analysis; and James Thurber's (1948) journalistic analysis.

Rudolf Arnheim (1944) did the only cross-sectional content analysis on the radio soap opera available to us today. He surveyed 43 serials on the air in 1941. He and his students covered 596 installments. This analysis is considered the classic study of broadcasting content and has provided the example for many of the television analyses that will be presented later in this chapter. It too can be faulted, however, as already noted. What we learn from it cannot be generalized to all soap operas, but rather only tells us about what was on the air during the season investigated. Still, it is very valuable as a basis for comparison with the modern soap opera (those on the air during the 1970s).

One other content analysis must be mentioned. In 1947, W. Lloyd Warner and William Henry analyzed one radio soap opera, *Big Sister*, combining content analysis of the serial itself with a content analysis of various projective tests given to listeners. Their approach was both anthropological and psychological. For them, soap operas were a form of folk literature representing "an idealized representation of human life — characters, emotion, and action" (Warner and Henry, 1948: 8). They believed that *Big Sister* functioned as a morality play.[2]

LOCALE

Most soap operas take place in the United States.[3] Except for excursions to foreign countries (more easily suggested in radio than television), the serials had and continue to have domestic settings, familiar to most listeners and viewers. In radio, rural settings were uncommon, as were settings in real cities such as Los Angeles or New York. Most were set in small or middle-sized towns with some vague geographical locale. In an analysis of 43 serials, Arnheim (1944) found that 8 took place in large cities, 16 in middle-sized or small towns, and 4 in rural areas. The remainder were combinations of large and small towns, institutions, or unspecified. *The Guiding Light,* for example, first took place in a small town called Five Points, later moved to another small locale, Selby Flats, and now takes place in Springfield.

Most television serials are still set in a middle-sized or small town. Mildred Downing (1974) notes that all serials were set "in the United States, and in a small town with a euphonious name, whose boundaries are amorphous and which seems to be located about 50 miles from New York, Chicago, or Los Angeles." Some current soaps are located in Pine Valley, Port Charles, Bay City, and Genoa City, all fictional. The newer soaps, however, are now located in large cities. *Ryan's Hope,* for example, is set in New York City, *Capitol* is located in Washington, D.C., and *Texas* in Houston.[4] In each of these soaps, though life is much the same as it is in the smaller towns, the trends to urban environments could be interpreted as a reflection of the population shift from rural to urban environments which has occurred in the United States in the last fifty years.

SEX ON RADIO AND TELEVISION

The subject of how sex is portrayed on the soaps has been the most controversial subject of all and the one that receives the most media attention (for example, People, 1982). The first point that must be made is that sexual acts are never shown on television and, of course, could only be imagined on radio. Instead, sexual acts are intimated, suggested by dramatic forms. "Petting," defined as kissing and fondling, can be shown on television but can only be suggested on radio. Most of what has been called "sex" on television actually concerns only intimations of sexual acts or (and the following is very important) their outcomes, such as crimes of passion, adultery (and other forms of infidelity), pregnancy, and abortion. Many of these appear regularly on television. On radio, sex was presented quite differently from the way it is shown on television. As we will show, questions about sex are morality questions.

Essentially, we are dealing with a time period when sexual morality in the United States has changed, and along with that change, there has been more emphasis on sexual acts in *all* entertainment programs. The Puritan morality of the nineteenth century was still very much in evidence in the 1930s when the soap opera was first introduced. As we write this book, however, some claim that puritanism is dead. To address the issue of a sexual revolution in the United States is beyond our scope. Only a few remarks will be made so that the material we present here and later in the chapter can be understood in context. There is general agreement that the radio soaps may have been titillating, but that the general tone was puritanical. People did divorce, and yet virginity before marriage was highly valued and sex outside of marriage was definitely taboo.

Arnheim (1944) does not consider sexual acts of any type in his content analysis, but he does consider morality, courtship, and marriage. From a more literary perspective, Stedman (1959, 1977) does consider sex as a topic. He draws heavily on James Thurber's (1948) report, also written in the 1940s. According to Thurber, sex was not presented realistically on the soaps. Following, from *The Beast and Me* (1948: 169), is Thurber's famous quote about sex and the radio soap opera:

> As for the sexual aspect of daytime morality, a man who had a lot to do with serials in the nineteen-thirties assures me that at that time there were "hot clinches" burning up and down the daytime dial. If this is so, there has been a profound cooling off, for my persistent eavesdropping has detected nothing but coy and impregnable chastity in the good women, nobly abetted by a kind of Freudian censor who knocks on doors or rings phones at crucial moments. Young Widder Brown has kept a doctor dangling for years without benefit of her embraces, on the ground that it

would upset her children if she married again. Helen Trent, who found that she could recapture romance after the age of thirty-five, has been tantalizing a series of suitors since 1933. (She would be going on fifty if she were a mortal but, owing to the molasses flow of soap-opera time, she is not yet forty.) Helen is soap opera's No. 1 tormentor of men, all in the virtuous name of indecision, provoked and prolonged by plot device. One suitor said to her, "After all, you have never been in my arms" . . . Helen, thereupon went into a frosty routine about marriage being a working partnership, mental stimulation, and, last and least, "emotional understanding." "Emotional understanding," a term I have heard on serials several times, seems to be the official circumlocution for the awful word "sex."

Stedman (1959) agrees that sex was deemphasized in the daytime serial drama. He says: "There were love scenes, but most were quite mild. Kissing was infrequent. In the radio serials a kiss was often merely suggested by a pause and a sigh." He notes that on television there was no ready way in which a kiss could be concealed. Because his analysis is so unsystematic, it is difficult to make generalizations, but he insists that sex on early television was far more realistic than on radio and that there was more of it. He reports on the March 27, 1958, episode of *The Secret Storm:* That episode opened with a woman kissing a man who was reclining on the sofa next to her. The man was a wayward husband and his friend, the "other woman." According to Stedman, the "good" people of the serials generally were not portrayed in such a manner.

Stedman also suggests that the early radio soap opera characters were naive, but by the time he was writing the naiveté about sex seemed to be disappearing even from the few radio soap operas left in 1959. The television soaps then on the air "demonstrated a much more mature attitude than was observed in the soap operas of the forties." He reports several incidents to make his point. For example, a woman on *As the World Turns* becomes pregnant and wears maternity clothes. An extreme example of frankness was reached on *Love of Life:* Co-heroine Meg had announced on April 14, 1958, that she was pregnant. This pregnancy did not please her, and two days later she declared that she would not have the baby, had found a doctor to help her with her "problem." The word "abortion" was not used, but the implication was clear.

Sex in the Modern Soap Opera

There is general agreement that sex is presented differently on the television soap opera than it was on radio. Gone are the pure and virginal women; premarital sex and adultery are common acts. What we do not know exactly is when that change occurred. No social scientist was very interested in the television soap opera until 1972 when Natan Katzman published his article. Katzman reported eight cases of marital infidelity, one bigamous marriage, four offspring of parents not married to each other, and various other romantic problems involving infidelity and premarital sex. Rose Goldsen (1977), in a study of soap operas in the first half of 1975, found eight divorces, two bigamous marriages, four married couples who had separated, six divorces being planned, and 21 couples who were not married either living or sleeping together. Two women had more than one bed partner, and several children had been born or conceived with their paternity in doubt.

Although there is no hard evidence, there does seem to be general agreement that sex was more prevalent on television in the 1970s than before that time. Not only do scholars and critics believe that soap operas are currently steamy, but all three networks use suggestive program promotions in both prime time and daytime to entice viewers. In particular, ABC's promotional theme of "Love in the Afternoon," broadcast regularly in the late 1970s and early 1980s, included sexual teasers.

Several investigators have tried to assess how much sex is actually shown on television (Greenberg et al., 1981; Fernandez-Collado et al., 1978; Franzblau et al., 1978; Greenberg et al., 1982; Silverman et al., 1978). These studies found that physically intimate behaviors — including kissing, embracing, petting, intercourse, and various discouraged sexual acts (such as exhibitionism and voyeurism) — occurred about one to three times per hour during prime time, depending on how late the hour. Sexual topics occurred more in the mid- than late seventies, when the overall frequency of sexual behavior decreased to one act per hour. Soap operas matched prime time in the number of sexual acts shown (and discussed) in the mid-seventies, then increased the sexual content while prime time decreased it. However, the most recent study of soaps, in 1978, suggests that the frequency of sexual acts had decreased to less than two per hour from earlier in the decade.

Prime-time television and daytime serials differ in the kind of sex portrayed and in the characters involved. Somewhat surprisingly, considering the advertisements and publicity given the soap operas, prime-time television is actually steamier than daytime television. During the mid- to late seventies, intercourse was the type of sex shown or referred to most frequently on prime time, while petting and kissing were most frequent on the serials. Although the frequency of intercourse on the soaps increased almost to equal that of petting in 1980, the latter still occurred more frequently during the five-year period from 1975 to 1980. Of course, explicit scenes of intercourse are not shown on television. Intercourse is implied by bedroom scenes and fades, morning-after scenes, or conversations. In contrast, petting is usually fairly explicit, with characters more likely to kiss than to talk about kissing. In both daytime and prime time, intercourse usually occurs between characters who are not married, while petting is almost as likely to occur between married as unmarried people. In addition, the soaps are more likely than prime time to show sex taking place between people who are married — again, a more conventional image. In the 1979 season, however, for each act involving married partners, there were more than two involving unmarried partners (Lowry et al., 1981). Thus, while the soaps may be tamer, both soaps and prime-time television seem to be presenting the message that intercourse without the sanction of marriage is common.

Moral Standards

Is this kind of sexual freedom acceptable behavior for soap opera characters? Research has not provided a clear answer, except for a related study on the treatment and resolution of moral violations in general (Sutherland and Siniawsky, 1982). These researchers studied a year of *Soap Opera Digest* (1980) synopses of *All My Children* and *General Hospital* (the most popular soaps among the younger audience), and coded these synopses for the "moral standards" that critics claimed were often violated in soaps:

(1) premarital/extramarital sex is wrong

(2) bigamy is wrong

(3) children should be born in wedlock

(4) abortion is wrong

(5) incest is wrong

(6) rape is wrong

(7) divorce must be carefully considered and not rushed into

(8) parents should not neglect their children

(9) children should obey their parents

(10) alcohol abuse/addiction is wrong

(11) drug abuse/addiction is wrong

(12) deception of others is wrong

(13) blackmail is wrong

(14) murder is wrong

They coded whether the violation was intended, attempted, or completed, whether the action was condoned by other characters or by social or economic sanctions, and the moral lesson in the conclusion.

The results generally suggested that soaps treat moral violations conventionally, that those who violate norms get punished. The most frequent moral violations on *All My Children* (36 episodes) and *General Hospital* (32 episodes) were deceit (about 29 percent), murder (24 percent), and premarital/extramarital sex (16.2 percent). Women were more likely to be deceivers, men more likely to be murderers, and both were equally likely to violate sexual morality. Most of the time (64 percent), violators' behavior was not condoned by others, and lessons in the plot resolution were overwhelmingly consistent with the critics' "moral standards." In other words, the soaps tend to support the status quo by ostracizing and punishing violators of moral standards.

Our comparison of prime-time with daytime drama shows that soap operas mention or feature sex about as often as on prime time but treat it differently. The soaps use sex as a serious plot element and linger on intimate action. Still, sex on soap operas remains largely within commonly held moral beliefs. Although we do not know if there is more or less sex on television than there was on radio, we do know that premarital sex and adultery are shown frequently on television and that such acts, although not condoned, are not punished as severely as they were on the radio soaps (Arnheim, 1944). By separating sex from other content areas, we have missed the deeper content. As we have shown, and will further specify, it is difficult to separate sex on television from the other social problems emphasized. We set this section off because it is here that the radio soaps differ so clearly from the television soaps. Soap operas have changed over time, and we suspect that nowhere has this change been more dramatic than in the presentation of sexual morality on daytime television serials as compared to their radio counterparts.

INTERPERSONAL RELATIONS AND SOCIAL ISSUES

Sex as a topic for study is important, but only as one aspect of the larger topic involving interpersonal relationships. For example, Mildred Downing (1974: 135) found that the bulk of serial time is devoted to romantic love, interpersonal relationships, and personal problems. She monitored 300 soap opera episodes in 1973 and found that 84 percent dealt with romantic love, 98 percent with interpersonal relationships, and 98 percent with personal problems. Obviously, all of these categories can occur together in one episode. In contrast, social problems received consideration in only 15 percent of the episodes, and community and/or world affairs in only 6 percent. Downing (1974) concluded:

> The world of the daytime serial is one in which romantic love, intense interpersonal relationships, and preoccupation with personal problems dominate — in fact, dictate — the action.

Issues such as job difficulties, money, and power were treated as extensions of personal problems.

In 1977, Greenberg and his colleagues (1982) updated Katzman's (1972) study of the main problems occurring on soaps. After coding several episodes of each soap then on the air, they found that more problems occurred per soap in 1977 and that slightly different problems were emphasized. Table 5.1 compares Greenberg's results with information that Arnheim collected in 1944 and Katzman's (1972) results to illustrate historical change in the soaps' major plot problems.

While the later soaps focused on many problems similar to those of their predecessors from the 1940s, most were more concerned with marriage, family, and medical problems than with social problems, the latter usually being work-related if they occurred at all. Overall, there was rela-

TABLE 5.1   Problems in Soap Operas (percentage)

Type of Problem	1941[1]	1970[2]	1977[3]
Marital	18	29	28
Family	10	12	22
Medical	9	24	16
Social	22	14	11
Romance	16	7	11
Crime	9	14	11
Other	16	0	0

1. Arnheim, 1944.
2. Katzman, 1972.
3. Greenberg et al., 1982.

tively little change in the types of plot problems that arose during the 1970s, although some new elements did appear in the situations with which characters were confronted.

> For marriage, infidelity was tops; for family, it was es-trangement among family members; for social, it was job-created difficulties; for crime, it was physically violent crimes; for romance, there was an even split in both sea-sons between difficulties in new romances and old ones. Only the origin of medical problems changed, with physi-cal disabilities more prominent in the 1970 study and mental illness more so in the 1977 soaps [Greenberg et al., 1982].

According to Greenberg et al. (1982), a number of new story elements derived from the prominence of sexual topics — sterility, abortion, sex-related crime — and the career-marriage conflict (a major thematic difference over time in *The Guiding Light* content — see next chapter).

Relationships are also the most common topic of characters' conversations, according to Greenberg and his colleagues. That characters discussed relationships especially, and then romance, seems quite reasonable, given the interpersonal focus of the soaps, and their conversations changed little between 1970 and 1977. Although "relevant" social issues could easily have been emphasized in serials of the 1960s, given the United States' social climate, they received scant attention (Downing, 1974). As noted earlier, only 15 percent of the episodes Downing studied discussed social problems, and only 6 percent discussed public affairs. While Downing's and Arnheim's coding systems differed, their research conclusions were similar. "The world of the serials," wrote Arnheim (1944: 47), is "quite clearly a 'private' world in which the interests of the community fade into insignificance." In 1978 Soares wrote that social issues were covered in soaps, but only those issues that were not too controversial and that could be treated on a personal basis. Plots were less concerned with the environment, politics, or homosexuality than with rape, abortion, drug abuse, alcoholism, wife beating and child abuse, or with health issues such as breast cancer and obesity. Soares's work was not conclusive, since it did not determine how common such issues were in story lines. However, Greenberg et al. (1982) suggest that socially relevant topics *have* increased in daytime serial plots. When they studied serials in 1977, Greenberg et al. (1982) found that the serials revealed more of a social issue orientation than in Katzman's (1972) study. They attributed much of this increase to a more open presentation and discussion of sex-related issues such as abortion, impotency, and infertility.

Violence and Crime

One effect of the importance of relationships to serial plots is their relative lack of violence. Violence is not infrequent on television, as numerous studies on prime-time and children's television have shown. Defining violence as "the overt expression of physical force (with or without a weapon) against self or others, compelling action against one's will on pain of being hurt or killed, or actually killing or hurting," Gerbner and Gross (1976) argue that violence is a simple dramatic form that provides cheap action for television while requiring little creativity from producers (also see Comstock, 1982b, for an overview of this issue).

They suggest that violence teaches the social rules of power in the United States by demonstrating who is weak, who is strong, and who can become an instrument for social control. One student research project compared the levels of verbal and physical violence on daytime serials and prime-time television. Five episodes each of five serials and a 20-hour sample of prime-time television were coded in June 1980. The results demonstrated clearly that soap operas were less violent than prime-time television and that they used violence in different ways.

Besides being less violent in general, soap operas rely more on verbal violence (77 percent of violent acts), while prime-time television relies more on physical violence (59 percent). In prime time, men hit and shoot other men who are likely to be strangers. On soaps, women and men argue and threaten each other, and the combatants are usually either lovers or family members. For this reason, soap opera violence also seems more realistic than that of prime time, since federal crime statistics suggest that most violent acts, such as murder, are committed by family members and friends rather than by strangers. Of course, soap opera characters engaged in violence are more likely to be related to each other anyway, simply because almost all characters on serials are. Few "strangers" visit serial families. Thus the relative infrequency of violence and their treatment of it distinguish the daytime serials from prime-time television.

Health

Another major theme of soap operas is health. Practically every serial on the air in 1982 had at least one character who was a doctor or nurse, and several soaps were set in hospitals, such as *The Doctors* and *General Hospital*. According to Mary Cassata and her colleagues (1979), sickness and injury are important and pervasive problems on soap operas. The coding of plot synopses in a 1977 *Soap Opera Digest* supported their contention — 42 percent of the characters mentioned had health problems. That most health problems beset characters between 22 and 45 is hardly surprising when we consider that most serial characters are in that age range. More important was the way in which characters developed such problems. Cassata et al. (1979) show that health problems were usually caused by accidents or violence, including car crashes and attempted murders or suicides.

Serials generally treat illness in ways that do not threaten their audiences. Many characters may develop serious illnesses, but few die from them. In all, 65 percent of the deaths on the soaps studied were due to accidents and violence, while disease caused 21 percent. In addition, Soares (1978: 23) notes that characters in soaps usually die of rare diseases that will probably never afflict audience members. In other words, disease and death are not presented in a threatening and/or realistic way.

Overall, daytime serials create a world dominated by interpersonal relationships, where characters discuss romantic, marital, and family problems, and where health and work are major concerns within these contexts. There is little physical violence or crime. The serial world seems physically safe but emotionally hazardous, mainly because of the continual sorting and re-sorting of relationships.

DEMOGRAPHY AND SOCIAL STATUS

By comparing the results of soap opera content analysis with information from the U.S. census, we can derive a surface-level picture of life in soap operas — especially in contrast to prime-time serials, which commentators see as less realistic than the soaps. Here the emphasis is on equality and inequality, not moral issues. The question we are asking is: Are men and women treated differentially, and if so, in what ways? We will be emphasizing work and, because the soap operas are about relationships, how men and women relate in conversations.

The Demography of Television

Using our analysis of cast lists for soap operas, as well as Nancy Signorielli's (1982) research, we can compare the demographics and occupations of serial and prime-time characters with population statistics from the U.S. census (see Table 5.2). On daytime serials, about half the major characters are male (very close to the U.S. census figures). In comparison, 60 to 80 percent of the prime-time characters are male, depending on the program (situation comedies involve more female characters than do crime or adventure programs).

Most people between the ages of 35 and 55 in the United States are married. This age range includes most television soap opera characters and also represents the largest age group in the United States. Unless otherwise designated, this analysis will focus specifically on that age range. About 15 percent of these people have been divorced, and the difference in the probability of divorce for men and women is slight. Yet serials, and especially prime-time television, show relatively few married characters. Some prime-time series simply neglect to inform viewers whether characters, particularly male characters, are married. According to Signorielli (1982), this is a major difference between male and female prime-time characters — one-third of the men's marital status is unknown, while women's marital status is almost always provided. This difference exists, if less noticeably, in daytime serials as well. Male characters seem less likely ever to have been married, and both sexes are less likely to be married currently than their real-life counterparts. Because soap opera plots are prone to focus on romance and family relations, marital status and divorce are appropriately more salient in daytime serials than on prime time. Yet almost half of all daytime serial characters (42 percent of the women, 46 percent of the men) have been or are being divorced — a much greater proportion than the 15 percent found in census figures. Thus, although soap operas may reflect the popula-

TABLE 5.2 Demographic Comparison of Men and Women Aged 35-55 (percentages)

| | Major Characters Who are Male | Percentage Married | | Labor Force Participation | | N |
		Men	Women	Men	Women	
Soaps[1]	50	60	70	98	76	328
Prime Time[2]	68	29	43	74	51	446
Census[3]	49	91	94	77	60	226,504,858

Note: The percentage of women in the work force varies by age. For all women it is 51.3 percent, but for the age range most heavily portrayed on television, this figure is more accurate.

1. Downing, 1974; Katzman, 1972; original content analyses of cast lists by S. Pingree.
2. Signorielli, 1982; Tedesco, 1974.
3. Signorielli, 1979; Waite, 1981.

tion more accurately than prime time and treat the sexes somewhat more equitably, neither daytime nor prime-time serials present a realistic picture of marriage in the United States.

The daytime serials also emphasize family relationships more than does prime-time television. Analysis of a five-day sample of prime-time shows, compared with the casts of eleven soap operas, revealed that the soaps had an average of six and one-half families per show, while the prime-time shows had one; however, the latter usually had more children.[5]

Work on Radio and Television

According to Raymond Stedman (1959: 40), the characters of daytime radio serials did not represent a wide cross-section of American society. In general, the principal characters were either housewives or professional people, and even the former were rarely stereotypical. For example, Mary Noble of *Backstage Wife* and Terry Burton of *The Second Mrs. Burton* had short but successful motion picture careers. Those soap operas which Stedman categorized as the Women Alone types were often about professional women. The main character of *Portia Faces Life* was a lawyer, while *Joyce Jordan, M.D.* started as an intern and graduated to become a full-fledged physician. The principal male characters were almost always professionals, usually doctors or lawyers. A few were barbers, farmers, or miners. No important character was an unskilled laborer.

Arnheim's (1944) more systematic analysis of radio soaps is similar to Stedman's. Again, most of the characters in the 43 serials analyzed in 1941 were either housewives or professionals. Because he does not break down the occupational categories by sex, there is no way to know whether any of the professionals were women, though a list of the serials analyzed reveals that some must have been, since *Portia Faces Life* was among those included in the analysis. Arnheim (1944: 40) writes that the complete absence of working-class characters is striking. He emphasizes that "there is no case of a factory worker, a miner, a skilled or unskilled worker playing an important role in any of the 43 serials sampled." That finding is puzzling, because in the years immediately preceding World War II, most of the men in the United States were either factory workers, farmers, or miners.

The radio soaps thus presented a distorted reflection of who worked at what. Although data are not available to compare the radio soaps with modern soaps (or with prime-time drama), there is evidence that such distortions still exist.

In the United States today, approximately 77 percent of the men and 60 percent of the women between the ages of 35 and 55 do market work. Prime time shows 74 percent of its male characters working (fairly accurate) but fails to show a proportional number of women in work roles. In contrast, daytime serials show 76 percent of their female characters and almost every male character in some sort of job. Not only do the serials show too many people working, but they show too many people in certain types of jobs. According to the census, only about 14 percent of the men and 15 percent of the women work as professionals, such as doctors, lawyers, teachers, nurses, and journalists. Although the number of professionals on prime time is close to the census figure, 46 percent of the daytime serials' male characters and 31 percent of their female characters are professionals. Most of the female professionals are nurses, entertainers, or journalists, while most of the male professionals are doctors and lawyers. The largest single work-related category for all female television characters is that of full-time homemaker: 23 percent of the daytime serials' women are homemakers, as are 24 percent of the prime-time women. Neither figure reflects the actual census figures regarding occupation.

In summary, the soaps exaggerate the number of people in the work force, and particularly the number of professionals, whereas prime-time series show too few women working but are reasonably accurate in the number of professionals. Finally, both types of programming exaggerate the differences between men's and women's employment levels.

More and more soap opera women have entered the labor force, just as more and more real women have done. Katzman (1972) found that in 1970, the working women in serials were mostly nurses and secretaries. Analyses of cast lists in 1980 (see Chapter 6 for *The Guiding Light's* cast lists) show substantial change in occupations for women, probably in response to women's increasing labor force participation and the women's movement. There were fewer serial homemakers in 1980 than in 1970, and fewer women worked in traditional women's jobs, such as nursing or secretarial positions. Meanwhile, the number of women shown working as doctors, lawyers, and business professionals increased substantially during the 1970s.

Simply knowing how many people are shown working on television reveals little about their work performance. The audience knows that Trapper John is a doctor and that Maggie Crawford is a lawyer, but how often do we actually see them working? How well do they perform their jobs? The results of several student content analyses, all supervised by Suzanne Pingree and using smaller and less diverse samples than some published content analyses, suggest answers to these questions. To determine how much work people actually do on soap operas, students coded one episode each of eleven different serials, noting the number of scenes in which characters were doing something clearly related to their occupation, such as a lawyer questioning a witness, or even "prop" work, such as shuffling papers in the background. Apparently, these serial characters seldom worked, performing such tasks in only 13 percent of the scenes studied. Men were shown working in twice as many scenes as women, a total of 16.8 percent.

Race, Age, and Class

Both daytime serials and prime time differ from the national census on several important demographic characteristics in addition to those already mentioned. About 97 percent of all daytime serial characters are white, and the rest mainly black (Greenberg et al., 1982), while some 87 percent of all prime-time characters are white (Signorielli, 1982). At the same time, from 70 to 80 percent of all daytime and prime-time serial characters are between the ages of 20 and 50; fewer than 16 percent of all daytime serial characters, and only 9 percent of prime-time characters, are older than 55 (Cassata et al., 1979; Signorielli, 1982). In both, only 6-10 percent of the characters are under the age of 20.

The upper and middle classes receive much more exposure from daytime serials than from prime time. According to one student research project, only 9 percent of all prime-time series portray members of the upper class, while more than one-quarter of all daytime serial characters are relatively well-to-do. In light of the fact that such people, defined as those with inherited wealth and listed in the social register, comprise only about 3 percent of the total U.S. population, it would seem that both types of programming tend to ignore the working class. Instead, prime-time television depicts mostly white adults, neither too young nor too old, and concentrated in the upper classes, while daytime serial characters are generally a bit older, a bit more white, and a lot more upper class than the rest of the television population.

SOAP OPERAS AND SEX ROLES: MAINTAINING THE STATUS QUO

Values

Despite the relative scarcity of full-time homemakers on serials, the values that the serials express tend to glorify and idealize women who are committed to children rather than careers. In one research project, students rated mothers in eleven serials for twelve characteristics associated with traditional or nontraditional behavior in order to determine whether characters were "good" or "evil" — an easy differentiation to make in this context, especially when another category, "weak," is added. Hypothesizing that "evil" characters would display non-sex-typed behavior, and that "good" characters would act traditionally, the students found exactly that. Conservative, nurturing women tended to be good characters, while evil women were career-oriented and nontraditional in their behavior. *All My Children*'s Erica Kane Martin, who informed her mother that she was a feminist (November 1, 1982, episode, and others), is the classic example of a selfish, ambitious, "bad" woman. This example suggests that the soaps equate "good" with traditional, sex-typed behavior; that is, a "good" woman is not career-oriented and ambitious.

Another project coded five network serials for frequency of prescriptive (ideological statements for others, advice), positive (calming behaviors in crisis, verbal praising, hopeful statements, physical affection), and negative (committing cruel or evil acts, lying) behaviors by mothers and "nonmothers." Nonmothers behaved positively or negatively, but seldom prescriptively; mothers were prescriptive and positive, never negative. Typical statements by serial mothers were: "I only want what's best for Joe, and I'm sure everything will go the way he wants it to," "Let's hope you find Laura because you two were made for each other, no matter what," and "I won't remain silent when something this wrong has been done." In contrast to women without children, mothers on daytime serials are benevolent and knowledgeable.[6]

In addition to the glorification of motherhood on the soaps, women are treated in other ways that reinforce stereotypical behavior. Marilyn Fine's (1981) study of conversations indicated a clear sex difference in the relationships of conversational partners. When women conversed with other women, they were usually related through family ties. When men conversed with men, they were usually professionals.

When women and men conversed, they were usually romantic partners. (That only men and women were romantic partners — all soap opera romance is heterosexual — suggests a rigid, stereotyped, unrealistic world.)

According to Turow (1974), men dominate most conversations in both daytime and prime-time serials. He coded instances of men and women on daytime and prime-time television giving advice or orders to the opposite sex and found that a strong sex-based division also occurred in the subjects for which men (or women) gave commands. Women gave advice and orders for "female" subjects, while men did so for both "male" and neutral subjects, such as "Close the door!" Still, male control of conversations was revealed in only 56 percent of the advice or orders given in daytime serials because so many soap opera topics are "female" (love, the family, home, and personal problems). If business were discussed more on daytime, conversations would resemble more closely those of prime time; that is, they would be dominated by "male" topics (business, law, government, crime, and coping with danger). As Turow (1974: 141) concluded:

> Television's dramatic landscape was shaped in such a way that the selection of characters, the assignment of occupations, and the movement of plots operated in concert to minimize the chances of women being given the opportunity to display superior knowledge with respect to men and to ensure that the areas in which they were given such opportunities were compartmentalized along traditional lines.

Although most television serials reflect the changes in women's work patterns that occurred during the 1970s, sex-typing occurred only slightly less often in 1982, according to a recent update of Turow's study. A sample of prime-time programs and daytime serials coded similarly to Turow's revealed that men continued to give most of the advice and orders on both soaps and prime time. Men also gave more advice for "female" topics — 51 percent of such advice in daytime serials, and 52 percent in prime time, almost equaling the amount given by women. While this implies more flexibility in sex role behavior, it might also imply increasing male domination of areas once secure for women, since changes in advising and ordering patterns are not necessarily changes in sex-typed behavior.

During the seventies there was a complementary change in the topics for which women gave commands. Turow (1974) learned that women in daytime serials gave only 20 percent of the advice and/or orders in business matters, while the 1982 analysis discovered women giving about 26 percent of such commands. Analysis of prime-time programming revealed a similar, though smaller, change. Men still gave most of the advice or orders, but sex-typed behavior had decreased slightly during the 1970s, especially for women. That serials portrayed a "traditional" world was reported by another student research project. Ideological statements were coded that either supported or defied traditional sex roles and values. Characters stated: "I guess I'm old-fashioned, but I think a wife's place is in the home"; "Why don't you stay home and do the housework, and I'll go out and earn the money?"; and "He's the master of the house now," which were defined as statements that supported traditional roles. A statement such as: "You don't need to be with your son all the time" (spoken to a mother) was coded as nontraditional. Universal statements in serials, though infrequent (less than one per episode), tended to support traditional sex roles. Also, although some serials show women in the work force and many in professional and nontraditional (male-dominated) occupations, most male-female interactions and their expressed value system still reveal a rigid, sex-typed world controlled by men. Nevertheless, the daytime serials of today tend to be less sex-typed than prime-time television.

CONCLUSION

Serials have more potential than prime time to present positive images of contemporary women, a potential similar to that of other forms of media designed for women, such as the women's pages of newspapers and women's service magazines. In 1978, Gaye Tuchman observed that women's writings could serve as a source of strength to the women's movement. Long and in-depth feature stories could appear in such a forum — the best type of context in which to discuss the social issues and problems central to changing sex roles. Serials focusing on relationships and family life could easily present more story lines and characters illustrating the harm caused by stereotypes and rigid sex roles. Women's magazines have presented more discussion of changing sex roles in their editorial and advice columns than in their fiction (Cantor and Jones, 1983), which for the most part has remained conservative. Yet soap opera writers have always contended that part of their mission is to teach the "lessons of life" to their listeners/viewers (Nixon, 1970; LeMay, 1982). The lessons they may be teaching, however, rarely concern the harm caused by stereotypes and rigid sex roles. Although we believe that soap operas follow social change in their messages rather than lead it, such a statement is too simplistic. All soap operas are not alike. For example, those that show women working outside the home are usually the ones that the press and others regard as the most traditional — *The Guiding Light, As the World Turns, Edge of Night.* Those that observers consider the most liberal — *The Young and the Restless, All My Children,* and *General Hospital* — show more sex and present more social problems but also show fewer women working outside the home.[7]

Overall, then, soap operas are another example of women's literature that supports the status quo regarding women's place in the social order. According to writers of most fiction targeted to women, women's concerns are the family, home, and social and sexual relationships. If one examines the proliferation of analyses of women's fiction in the last decade, that contention is well documented. There seems to be a more liberating message about sex behavior per se than about sex roles in particular. As we show in the following chapter, women's concerns in soap operas, and possibly other fiction as well, are changing somewhat as many women leave a family-centered world to become an integral part of the work world.

NOTES

1. Drawing on Goffman's frame analysis, Gaye Tuchman (1979), strongly suggests that by viewing the media as frames providing ensembles of texts, it is possible to discuss the media and their contents as myths. She defines myths as "ways of seeing the world that resonate with the conscious mind and the unconscious passions that are embedded in, expressions of, and reproduce social organization." In other words, Tuchman and others (for example, McCormack, 1982) believe that a more structural analysis will shed light on the questions of change and persistence that cannot be answered fully by the data already collected.

2. Thelma McCormack (1982) puts this study, along with Arnheim's, into a sociology of knowledge perspective and provides a critique of content analysis from an historical perspective.

3. Prime-time series, serials, and movies vary so widely in their locales that to compare them to soap operas is not appropriate.

4. *Texas* was canceled on December 31, 1982, but was still on the air when this book was in progress. See Chapter 2 for more details.

5. Here and elsewhere in this book, we will occasionally refer to students' research projects. These projects were conducted by students in Suzanne Pingree's courses at the University of Wisconsin — Madison. They were small in sample size, but otherwise rigorous. We include them to suggest how students and other investigators might carry out further research. They are not meant to be conclusive, but are presented as examples of projects that students and others can conduct.

6. Rose Goldsen (1977) suggests that children are not valued on soaps because they rarely appear, often die young, and are otherwise neglected.

7. Suzanne Pingree investigated ways to array soaps on a traditional-to-nontraditional scale. She found that the problem is multidimensional, as we have reported here. For further details concerning methodology and definitions, one may contact Pingree at the University of Wisconsin.

6

THE GUIDING LIGHT, 1948-1982

This chapter contains original research, a content analysis of radio and television scripts of *The Guiding Light,* the only soap opera still on the air that was first broadcast on radio and then continued on television. This analysis emphasizes the differences between radio and television programs and shows how social relations, work, and conversational topics have changed in the past 35 years.

This chapter, consisting of an in-depth analysis of *The Guiding Light* (Irna Phillips, originator), provides an example of how a given soap opera can change over time. *The Guiding Light* is the ideal soap opera for such an analysis, as it has been broadcast for the longest period of time and has continued to engage viewers throughout its history. The first episode was broadcast on radio in 1937. The show was dropped briefly in 1941, but some 75,000 letters of protest forced the sponsor to reinstate it. In 1952, *The Guiding Light* began on television, though it continued on radio until 1956. It is the only radio soap opera that was transferred to television.

Throughout the 45 years it has been on the air, characters have married, loved, disappeared, died, or simply drifted out of the story line. Originally, it was about the life of a minister (Dr. Ruthledge) and his family. In the late 1940s, the central family, the Bauers, of the present serial appeared, and the story moved its locale from Five Points to Selby Flats. It now takes place in Springfield.

This discussion of content change is based on an analysis performed by Debra Mies (1982), who examined *Guiding Light* scripts that spanned three decades, specially those broadcast in March/April 1948, 1958, and 1968. In addition, she video-taped and coded the actual programs broadcast during March 1982. A summary of the plots and story lines over *The Guiding Light*'s broadcast history is available elsewhere (LaGuardia, 1974); the emphasis here is on the messages being communicated concerning work and social relationships.

AN OVERVIEW

Table 6.1 shows the major characters and their assigned occupation in each year studied. The characters' importance was determined by the number of conversations in which they participated during each episode.

Almost twice as many characters appeared on *The Guiding LIght* in 1982 as in 1948. The increase can be attributed to two factors: The radio soaps were only 15 minutes long, while the television serial is one hour long; in addition, the action involved fewer story lines in 1948. The 1948 cast was not evenly divided between men and women as in later years (60 percent men in 1948, in comparison with 55 percent in 1958 and 1968, and 50 percent in 1982), and only the 1948 cast included a minister as a major character. That year, the story still retained much of the religious flavor that had been the show's hallmark when Dr. Ruthledge and his family were the main characters.

Most of the male characters have always been shown as employed. In 1948, all males worked. In 1958 and 1968, retired Papa Bauer and two children, Bob Wiley and Mike Bauer, were the only males who did not work. All 1982 males worked. In addition, most have always had high-status, well-paying positions. Different professions came to be emphasized over time. Positions were business-oriented in

1948, doctor-lawyer oriented in 1959 and 1968, and divided between business and the professions in 1982.

As might be expected, the female characters' work activities were quite different. In 1948, two of the four women worked outside the home, one as a nurse and the other as a radio star with very mixed feelings about her career. In a scene with her husband, Charlotte Brandon states that her radio work is not her true career. Rather:

> A cake to bake, and a floor to sweep, and a tired child to sing to sleep. What does a woman want more than this — a home, a child, and a man to kiss [Friday, April 16, 1948].

In 1958, only one woman worked outside the home, though one other, Marie Grant, earned some money from her paintings. By 1968, two of the five adult female characters were full-time housewives. The rest worked in traditionally "female" occupations — one as a store clerk, the others as nurses. The situation was very different by 1982, when Bert Bauer was the only full-time housewife. All other characters worked at least occasionally outside the home. Taking a hiatus from housework, Hope Spaulding redesigned the interior of Mark Evans's apartment. Bea Reardon cooked and cleaned for her boarders as well as her family. Besides a clear shift toward showing working women on *The Guiding Light*, there was an even sharper change in the types of work performed by female characters. In 1948, the ambivalent Charlotte Brandon was the only woman who worked outside of the stereotyped traditional occupations for women. In 1982, by comparison, two females were cast as business executives and one as a graphic designer. These three characters, as well as the one nurse in the story (Hillary Bauer), all valued their careers. The soap opera in 1982 focused away from family matters and toward business, for both women and men. That emphasis on business is reflected in both their occupations and conversations.

TABLE 6.1 Cast of Characters and Their Occupations

Male	Female
1948	
Dr. Matthews — minister	Susan Collins — housewife
Martin McClain — wealthy oil industrialist	Julie Collins — housewife
Roger Collins — business executive in training	Charlotte Brandon — radio star
Ray Brandon — law clerk, law student	Pam Hale — nurse
Ralph Fleming — lawyer	
Ted White — radio producer	
1958	
Paul Fletcher — doctor	Bert Bauer — housewife
Dick Grant — doctor	Marie Grant — housewife/artist
Bill Bauer — public relations	Robin Holden — child (student)
Papa Bauer — retired	Meta Bauer — housewife
John Lipsey — pharmacist	Marian Winters — nurse
Dr. Gaynor — doctor	Trudy Bauer — housewife
Bruce Banning — doctor	
Dr. Meyers — doctor	
Bob Wiley — child (student)	
Mike Bauer — child (student)	
Mark Holden — construction/designer	

1968

Ed Bauer — doctor
Bill Bauer — public relations
Mike Bauer — lawyer
Marty Dillman — law student
Joe Werner — doctor
John Fletcher — child (student)
Papa Bauer — retired
George Hayes — lawyer
Dr. Jackson — doctor
Dean Freeman — dean of law school
Paul Fletcher — doctor

Leslie Bauer — housewife
Peggy Scott — nurse
Bert Bauer — housewife
Tracy — store clerk
Hope — child
Student Nurse

1982

Ross Marler — lawyer
Mike Bauer — lawyer
Mark Evans — business executive
Floyd Parker — musician, hospital engineer
Quentin McCord — archaeologist
Ed Bauer — doctor
Tony Reardon — nightclub manager
Henry Chamberlain — business executive
Josh Lewis — business executive

Amanda Wexler — business executive
Carrie Marler — graphics designer
Vanessa Chamberlain — business executive
Hope Spaulding — housewife (interior designer)
Maureen Reardon — secretary
Hillary Bauer — nurse
Nola Reardon — housekeeper, assistant
Bea Reardon — housewife/boarding house manager
Bert Bauer — housewife

TABLE 6.2   Message Types (percentages)

	1948	1958	1968	1982
Values	59%	32%	22%	15%
Family/Relationships	18	38	33	40
Doctors/Health	6	13	30	22
N	98	68	60	60

CONVERSATION ANALYSIS

After coding characters' conversations for "truths" — messages about life, priorities, and values, Mies learned that in 1948, "Life and death walk hand in hand at all times." A 1958 character warned that "everybody needs to be needed." In 1968, one intoned: "There can be success even in failure." Another concluded in 1982: "I like the fact that you won't make a commitment unless you're going to fulfill it." Three message types, varying in emphasis, were thus distinguished at each of the four periods studied (see Table 6.2).

The 1948 messages overwhelmingly concerned values — statements such as: "Chance is direction that we neither see nor understand" or "Kitchen and home are a girl's whole kingdom." Many of these lessons were delivered by the minister, who was involved in more conversations than any other character. In 1958, family and relationship messages surpassed value statements in frequency. Characters stated: "Having a father who loves and needs you — it is a wonderful thing" and "Someone who loves children the way she does — loves doing things for them — she should have a houseful." This trend continued in 1968. "Since when is business more important than marriage?" asked one character. "She needs real family life. I had an apartment and a housekeeper but it's not the same — family is family, you know," declared another. Meanwhile a message type infrequent before 1968 became almost as important — those about medical issues, including doctors and health. Characters stated that

TABLE 6.3 Message Content (percentages)

	1948	1958	1968	1982
Universal/Audience	45%	43%	47%	40%
About Men	29	40	38	25
About Women	26	18	18	35
N	98	68	60	60

"medicine needs good surgeons," and "He should have learned that he's an excellent surgeon but he's not God."

By 1982, family and relationship messages dominated content, and characters such as the recently divorced Maureen Reardon said: "I wanted to keep our relationship fresh and thought a baby would tie us down. But I woke up one morning and I saw how empty our lives were. Because we'd never made plans for the future. I think children are the future." Classes of messages changed as well, according to Mies (1982) (see Table 6.3).

In each year *The Guiding Light* was studied, messages were usually delivered as what Mies (1982) calls "universals" — statements made to the audience more than to or about other characters in the story. In each year except 1982, men were the second most frequent referent.

Specific meanings or values conveyed in messages also changed. From the 1940s through the 1960s, any career-marriage conflict was between wife and husband over the husband's dedication to his career. As Leslie Bauer lamented: "I guess all wives fight a losing battle with a mistress as demanding as medicine." By 1982, career-marriage conflicts were also provoked by a woman's career interfering with her marriage or her ability to find a suitable spouse. Executive Amanda Spaulding is told constantly that what she really needs is a good man. The few medical messages that were delivered in 1948 and 1958 emphasized how doctors' careers affected their personal lives. In 1968, such messages also stressed the societal importance of good doctors. Recent medical messages included mental health issues important to medicine. Two related themes treated consistently in *The*

TABLE 6.4   Location of Speaker by Message Content (percentages)

	1948		1958		1968		1982	
	home	work	home	work	home	work	home	work
Friends	72%	28%	48%	52%	100%		34%	66%
Business				100	14	86	25	75
Romance	100		100		100		32	68
Family	100		100		90	10	80	20
N	183	32	137	121	177	33	110	173

Guiding Light were honesty and communication. Apparently, only honest people who communicate fully with others are happy and successful in life.

Mies (1982) also coded conversations for where a character was speaking and about what (within a set of discrete categories). As Table 6.4 shows, the once rigid separation of public and private affairs has become progressively blurred in the soap world. In the early days, business was not discussed at all, probably because the soaps were usually set at home or in unknown locales. Relationships — family, friends, and romance — were only discussed at home. In 1958, friends spoke to each other as often at work as at home. In 1968, some business was discussed at home, but the pattern persisted that matters of feeling were for home and matters of business for the workplace. In 1982's *Guiding Light,* some important changes can be discerned. A great deal more of everything was discussed at work — in offices, hospitals, restaurants — than ever before (something true, no doubt, of other soap operas as well).

A second way of looking at this movement from the private to the public sphere is to examine where women and men speak in dyads. Table 6.5 shows a similar pattern over time to the previous table, revealing that 1982 was a different, less stereotyped year for *The Guiding Light.* Up until then, home was the only place where women talked to each other, and it was also where most male-female interactions occurred. In contrast, men's interactions became more evenly divided between home and work. Over the period studied,

TABLE 6.5 Speaker Dyads by Location (percentages)

	1948		1958		1968		1982	
---	home	work	home	work	home	work	home	work
MF	100%		64%	36%	98%	2%	40%	60%
MM	57	43%	17	83	39	61	23	77
FF	100		100		100		44	56
N	168	32	121	118	169	30	102	170

then, the world was more rigidly divided for women than men until 1982, when women clearly moved out of the home.

Women's and men's relationships have also changed over time. Mies (1982) found that males have almost always interacted with other males in business relationships. Females usually interacted with female friends until 1982 when, like males, they too began to interact in business relationships. In 1968, male-female interactions emphasized romance over friendship, while in 1982 business and romance were represented equally (see Table 6.6).

Romantic relationships were exclusively heterosexual for all time periods, supporting similar results of Marilyn Fine's (1971) study.

Finally, conversation topics differed by year (see Table 6.7).

Dialogue Samples

In 1948, personalities and feelings were the most common topics, as shown in the following samples.

Martin McClain: Do you know the stress and strain upon the mind and heart of a man who is guilty as I'm guilty — who for years sought to escape from his thoughts, from his conscience, through work and the gaining of power and more power? No.

No, you wouldn't know. I have suffered through the years as only a man can suffer who has destroyed. I want to — do

TABLE 6.6 Speaker Dyads by Type of Interaction (percentages)

	1948				1958				1968				1982			
	bus	fam	rom	frnd	bus	fam	rom	frnd	bus	fam	rom	frnd	bus	fam	rom	frnd
MF	13%		36%	51%	9%	16%	19%	56%	1%	21%	58%	19%	33%	14%	31%	23%
MM		33		67	55	17		28	54	46			71	16		13
FF				100				100	17	28		56	51	39		10
N	64		53	113	58	36	26	117	32	62	92	41	123	55	54	55

TABLE 6.7   Topics of Conversation, by Year

Topic	1948	1958	1968	1982
Romance	11%	14%	28%	15%
Family/Friend Relationships	16	16	18	13
Business/Careers	13	20	12	33
Home/Social	2	18	6	8
Health	11	4	10	14
Personality	25	23	17	16
Religion	3	—	—	—
Feelings	19	4	9	1
Total	100%	99%	100%	100%
N	369	307	245	427

something about that. If it can be done — without Susan knowing her father for what he is, I'll be grateful.

Another example:

Dr. Matthews: That man must have lived a horrible life during all these years. Sending a man to prison unjustly as he did —

Ralph Fleming: How little we know of people, Dr. Matthews. Martin McClain — a name, a big name in the oil industry — a name that anyone would think would bring with it all that was good in life.

Dr. Matthews: Yes, how little we know of people. How little we know of conscience. Somehow I think that's what killed Mr. McClain, really — conscience and fear, fear of — of many things, of many people.

In 1948 the infrequent conversations about work most often concerned Charlotte Brandon's uncertainty about choosing radio work as her true career. Although topics were not distinctly sex-segregated, women and men did tend to discuss romance in their conversations together more often that did men or women separately.

In 1958, personalities, business, and home were the topics most commonly discussed. One home-oriented conversation opened with Marie Grant and Bert Bauer of

"Two Easter Eggs, One Painted Like a Pirate and the Other a Soldier":

> *Bert:* Marie, you really made these yourself?
>
> *Marie:* Of course I did.
>
> *Bert:* Well, I know you're a very talented artist and all that but— and how did you get chocolate fudge inside them?
>
> *Marie:* You break a little of the shell at one end, stick a pin in the other end and blow the egg out.
>
> *Bert:* Blow —?
>
> *Marie:* (nods her head) Very simple. Then you put sticky paper where the pinhole was and fill the shell with hot fudge. When it gets hard, you paint the face.

Home-oriented conversations between men and women in 1958 also considered social arrangements and decisions about where to live. Stereotyped relationships between speakers and locations where women and men had conversations seem even more rigid than in 1948. In 1958, women and men conversed mostly about romance and personalities; the most frequent conversation topic among men was business, and among women, relationships in families and with friends. Contrast the following conversations, the first involving two doctors:

> *Dick:* I wish you could have seen what I saw this morning.
>
> *Paul:* What was that?
>
> *Dick:* Dr. Meyers did a stomach resection.
>
> *Paul:* I'm an internist, not a surgeon, remember?
>
> *Dick:* That wouldn't have kept you from appreciating this. It was really a masterpiece.

The second conversation involves a doctor and nurse (a much rarer form of business conversation, since most were between men).

Dick: Well, there's another of Dr. Meyers' patients coming in next Monday who'll need private nurses. (to Marian) The doctor told me to see if you could take the case.

Marian: Well, I — I don't know, Dr. Grant . . .

Dick: Has your registry signed you for something else?

Marian: No, but — well, I just can't give you an answer yet.

Dick: We'll have to know within a day or two.

Marian: Yes I — please don't misunderstand, Dr. Grant, I appreciate your asking me to take another case —

Finally, from 1958, two men discussed another's personality.

John: I didn't pay much attention to them (rumors) until I heard it from Dr. Gaynor too.

Paul: Oh — that guy.

John: What've you got against him, Paul?

Paul: I don't have anything against him, I just think he's an overgrown spoiled kid. Always had too much for his own good.

Conversations in 1968 shifted away from personalities to family, friendships, and especially romances. These conversations were more often the subject when two women talked, yet men and women discussed relationships as well, and not necessarily their own.

Leslie: Joe, I — I can't preach sense to Ed — how can I help? What can I do for a man I love very much?

Joe: By all means, don't preach — let him alone.

Leslie: I can't do that, either, Joe, I love him. I love him as a man — and I know that as a man he must be happy — and proud — as a surgeon.

Joe: Maybe the answer is — make him forget the surgeon for tonight. Make him remember the man. Make him know you're his woman. Maybe it's as simple as that.

Men also discussed their romances:

Ed: Wasn't there a girl you were pretty crazy about?

Mike: She was married — still is, I imagine. I walked out of her life and I closed the door.

Ed: Can't that door be opened?

Mike: I don't want to open it. She and I were never meant to be.

Ed: Okay. Then I can introduce you to some awfully attractive nurses.

Mike: Don't bother — I can handle my own social life.

Ed: Don't you want to get married again?

Mike: I'm not anxious.

Ed: Dad would like you to — at least that's what Mom tells me.

Mike: Dad's told me the same thing — but I'm going to be very careful not to fall in love for a long time to come.

In 1968, romance dominated conversations — the most frequent topic for women and men among women, and tied with business as the second most frequent type among men. By a slight margin, health was the most frequent topic among men in 1968. Because so much content was about doctors and medical treatment, many health conversations could probably be classed as business talk instead.

More conversations dealt with business topics in 1982 than in any of the other years studied, and more conversations occurred in business than in home settings. For example:

Amanda: Vanessa, we were just talking about a message that Mark gave to Ross that somehow got misplaced.

Mark: You know, I also gave Vanessa a message several times when I called.

Amanda: Oh, I never heard that either, but I guess Vanessa has been very busy planning the stockholders' meeting.

Vanessa: Oh, yes, it's been frantic. Darling, I'm terribly sorry, I know you asked me to give your regards to people here, but I'm afraid that with the mad dash I just wasn't able to unless I'd spoken to her right after I'd spoken to you.

Amanda: Well, that's funny, Vanessa. I can remember being at the Hide Out with Jennifer one night when you talked with Mark behind the bar.

Vanessa: You're right, you were. Oh, I'm sorry. Well of course that was the night I was so worried about my father. I'm sorry.

Amanda: Well, it's not really that important, anyway. My decorator is almost finished with my house, so I want to confirm the cocktail party on the evening before the annual stockholders' meeting. So, Vanessa, will you be so kind as to call all the major stockholders personally and invite them.

Ross, you're also invited of course, with Carrie.

Ross: Thank you very much and we will be there.

Amanda: Mark, I'm going to introduce you as our new advisor in foreign affairs. So I would appreciate it if you'd make up an informal report to give on the opening day of the meetings.

Mark: I'd be glad to, Amanda.

Amanda: One last thing. I want everyone prepared for a news item about to break.

Overall, analysis of 1982 content reveals several major shifts. The major topic of conversation between women and men became business, not romance. Not only were more than half of all conversations between men only about business, but business also became a major conversational topic between women. Thus 1982 emerges as a year in which traditional stereotypes about women's behavior and their attachment to the home-sphere in favor of the outside world were increasingly challenged.

SUMMARY

Before 1982, *The Guiding Light* had never portrayed a truly career-oriented woman. The serial has always been a family saga, and its messages, as we have shown, have traditionally centered around family and marriage. Several characters, notably Charlotte Brandon, implied that woman's true vocation is the home. It would undoubtedly be informative to analyze the 1970s, which produced female characters comfortable in their careers in 1982. That change, from home-centered to business-centered is an example of how the soaps have changed in fifty years. Of course, many other aspects remained relatively constant. Although never again as important as in 1948, values still accounted for 15 percent of all 1982 messages. Health, and especially relationship, continued to comprise a significant portion of soap opera messages. For many years the soaps consistently promoted particular message types for their audiences. That consistency of values likely reflects Irna Phillips's attitude toward the soaps (see Chapter 3), and The Guiding Light's current writers continue to structure stories around family relationships and interactions.

The Guiding Light moved from an introspective and inwardly oriented world in 1948, one focusing on feelings and personalities, to a sex-segregated world of business and home in 1958, to a world where both sexes were concerned with romantic relationships in their separate settings in 1968, to one where women and men both focus on business in a much more open social environment.

It is unfortunate that more analyses of this type have not been done. We do not know much at all about the other radio soaps. Also, it is unfortunate that information from the 1970s is absent. For example, what looks like a reemphasis on the family in 1982 after a decline in 1968 instead may have been a decline from a 1970s peak. Of course, the absence of data from this crucial decade is not the only reason for treating the results of these analyses cautiously; ten-year intervals may not be sufficiently sensitive to pick up changes, one month from each period may not adequately represent the period, and so on. However, this study represents a first attempt to provide some measure of systematic study to the history of soaps — other studies have relied on story lines and nonrandom examples to illustrate the author's subjective conclusions. Perhaps other investigators will be inspired to conduct more systematic and less subjective studies of the archive of soap scripts and/or tapes (both video and audio) so that these findings can be supported, amplified, or even refuted.

7

SOAP OPERA AUDIENCES

The changing audience. Who watches; why they watch. How viewers use the soaps. The effects of soap operas on behavior, beliefs, attitudes, and knowledge.

Mass communication research has centered primarily on the audience. Three kinds of studies are common: demographic studies, which describe audience characteristics; surveys and interview studies, to find out why people watch television and how it gratifies them; and studies that look at the ways in which television affects individual viewers. In the three sections that follow, each of these topics will be explored separately.

DEMOGRAPHIC AND DESCRIPTIVE STUDIES

The Radio Audience

As emphasized throughout, the soap opera was developed for the housewife audience, though the sponsors and networks were never sure which women were listening to the programs. Ratings were conducted through telephone polls during the early days of the radio, but these polls consistently underestimated the size of the audience, since many households in the United States did not have telephones in the 1930s but did have radios. As the decades passed, polling became scientific, and by the time the soap opera left radio, sponsors had a relatively satisfactory idea of the size and demographic characteristics of the audience. The only in-depth picture of the radio audience comes from studies done by the Office of Radio Research (ORR) at Columbia University. The ORR was created in 1937 by a grant from the Rockefeller Foundation "to study what radio means in the lives of listeners." The director of the ORR was Paul Lazarsfeld, considered by some to be the founder of communication research in the United States. The studies conducted by that group resulted in the classic research reports by Herta Herzog (1944) and Helen Kaufman (1944).

Helen Kaufman (1944: 86) reports on results from two surveys, both conducted through personal interviews. The total sample from these surveys was "10,000 women in all walks of life." About one-half of these interviews were obtained from urban women throughout the United States, and the others were from both urban and rural women in Iowa. Because of the sample selected, there were no data about the men in the audience, if any.

The results show that soap opera listeners were no different from nonlisteners in some characteristics but somewhat different in others. For example, listeners were not more isolated socially (as many at the time believed). They did differ, however, in socioeconomic characteristics. There were about one and a half as many listeners among farm women as among women living in metropolitan areas. Although both listeners and nonlisteners read approximately the same amount, their preferred types of reading material differed. Soap opera listeners, who were likely to be less educated than nonlisteners, were apt to read more "highbrow" magazines. Overall, the findings from these studies and other reports show that while soap opera listeners existed in every social and cultural group, they were more likely to be from small towns and rural areas, of lower educational attainment, and of lower socioeconomic status when compared to the nonlistener.

When audiences for different programs were analyzed,

the content of the programs seemed to make a difference. For example, *Ma Perkins* appealed particularly to low-educated rural women. In contrast, *The Guiding Light* listeners were more evenly divided among several socioeconomic groups. According to Kaufman (1944: 104), the two programs appeared to provide different types of gratification. *Ma Perkins* was the story of a woman alone, running both a business and a home. Her accomplishments, trials, and tribulations — the way she was frequently misunderstood and finally appreciated — allowed for pleasant wishful thinking, especially among women of similar background. In contrast, *The Guiding Light* appealed to a more middle-class audience, the members of which, Kaufman said, were "puzzled and worried."

Evidence indicates that differences in the audience composition of individual series existed, but that these differences were not outstanding. Listeners tended to stay tuned to a particular network or station and therefore listened to a chain of programs. However, there is also evidence that programs drew audiences and that listeners were often selective, choosing programs rather than stations. *Ma Perkins* and *The Guiding Light* followed each other for a while on NBC Blue, but their overlap in audience was only 40 percent. Other programs broadcast in a chain had a higher degree of audience retention.

Ratings and Audience

From the beginning of sponsorship, the networks and advertising agencies used ratings to ascertain audience size and composition. The first rating system was developed by Archibald Crossley, an opinion researcher (Mankiewicz and Swerdlow, 1978). The most successful early system, originated by Claude Hooper, employed "checkers" — 1500 women in 36 cities (Thurber, 1948). Checkers measured the audience of a given serial by telephoning as many people as they could reach while the serial was being broadcast. Although this form of sampling would be considered unscientific now, the results were taken seriously by sponsors. The system now in use was developed by A. C. Nielsen. It was widely adopted by the middle 1940s and had many advantages over the Hooper system. From its inception, the Nielsen organization used the audimeter, a device attached to the radios in households across the country. This device automatically registers the hours a set is on and records the various programs selected. By 1944, audimeters were used nationwide, distributed to a cross-section of households in cities, towns, and rural areas. Although the Nielsen system has been both criticized and defended (see Cantor, 1971, 1980), it had clear advantages over the Hooper system, which used a biased sample selection process and depended on the reports of listeners.

The Television Audience

Since television became a mass medium in the 1950s, A. C. Nielsen Co. has continued to provide audience data to advertisers and broadcasters. The Nielsen sample currently consists of 1150 households selected nationally. Through computer connections, records are obtained which inform analysts when the television set is on, which channel is tuned in, and when a channel is changed. These data do not provide information about viewers' reactions to programs, how many household members are viewing at any one time, or whether the programs "affect" viewers. A. C. Nielsen provides subscribers with specific numerical information, all estimations and statistical projections, not absolute numbers. The data provided through ratings tell subscribers to the service what percentage of all United States households are tuned in to a particular program at a specific time. Ratings are important, because the higher the rating, the more the networks can charge the advertisers for the commercial

TABLE 7.1   Rank of Daytime Serials: August 2-6, 1982

Rank and Serial Title	Rating	Share
1. All My Children	9.9	32
2. General Hospital	9.5	33
3. One Life to Live	8.4	30
4. The Young and the Restless	8.2	30
5. As the World Turns	7.5	25
6. The Guiding Light	7.3	25
7. Ryan's Hope	7.0	26
8. Days of Our Lives	6.4	20
9. Capitol	5.8	21
10. Another World	4.9	17
11. Edge of Night	4.3	15
12. Texas	3.1	13
13. Search for Tomorrow	3.1	11
14. The Doctors	2.4	9

Note: Data provided by A. G. Nielsen Co. NTI Preliminary Estimates.

television time being purchased. Daytime ratings are far lower than prime time for network shows, because fewer television sets are turned on. Still, the highest-rated shows not only get more advertising support, but advertisers pay more for their spots. For example, the soap operas on ABC have consistently received high ratings during the last five years. Thus, ABC shows are better funded, a fact reflected in the quality of their productions. Table 7.1 shows how the soap operas on the air during the summer of 1982 ranked by ratings.

Other information provided by A. C. Nielsen is also important to the networks, advertisers, and producers, in particular the share and the audience demographics. The share is the percentage of the households that have their sets on and tuned to a particular channel during a specific time period. A show can have a rating of 10 but a share of 30, meaning that 10 percent of all homes in the United States have their sets turned to a particular program, with 30 percent of all sets on at the same time. The most useful data for social science purposes are the demographics. Demographics tell broadcasters what proportion of their share of the audience is young or old, black or white, rich or poor, and in addition provides information about where the audience lives. The most important information to advertisers is the sexual composition of the adult audience. Nielsen data do not report the sex designation of the children under 12 in the audience.

Many have criticized the Nielsen methods because of the small size of the sample. Each household represents approximately 66,000 families. Also, because only households are sampled, the data collected may not accurately reflect the total viewing audience. For example, people who may watch television in the workplace, college dormitories, and institutions. Thus, by only measuring those who view at home, some people (and especially the daytime audience) may be missed. Journalistic and impressionistic reports indicate that there are a number of viewers who do watch one or more soap operas outside the home — workers and college students (ABC, n.d.). (Students in the audience will be discussed below.)

Changes in the Television Audience

In 1970, A. C. Nielsen reported that 20 million viewers watched one or more soap operas on the average each day. That audience consisted of mostly women 18 years and older (76 percent of the total). The remaining 24 percent were divided among men over 18 (15 percent), teenagers 12-17 (about 5 percent), and the remainder children 2-11 (Katzman, 1972).

In 1981, the figures showed little change. There were fewer women 18 and older, down from 76 to 70 percent, and a slightly larger proportion of men and teenagers. The total size of the reported audience remained approximately the same as it was in 1970 (World Almanac, 1982).

These figures also point out that the proportion of the total population watching daytime network television has declined substantially since 1970 (Broadcasting, 1977). In 1970 there were approximately 60 million homes with television in the United States, and in 1980 the number increased to 80 million due to the increased number of adults in the population. Those born during the baby boom years (1947-1953) had reached adulthood, and many had established households. One would think that as the number of households increased, so would the size of the daytime audience. However, because of the alternative viewing opportunities offered by cable television, video-tape recorders, and UHF stations, and because so many women are now in the work force, the potential audience is in fact proportionately smaller than it was in 1970. Still, soap operas are the most popular shows on during the daytime hours, consistently getting the highest share of the available audience. Moreover, as can be seen from the chart above, some soap operas are very popular and command a large share of the available audience. During the summer of 1981, for example, *General Hospital* had 14 million viewers — over 40 percent of the available daytime audience. Not only are some shows more popular than others, but the demographic characteristics of the audience vary among shows. In addition, shows that were highly rated in 1971 are now less popular, while low-rated 1971 shows are now the most popular. The key factor for this change has already been discussed. The highest-rated shows are now on ABC because that network consciously strove for and succeeded in attracting viewers by making their soap operas trendy and often sensational (Business Week, 1979).

Two highly rated shows in 1971 were *As the World Turns* and *The Guiding Light*. The two highest-rated shows in 1981 were *General Hospital* and *All My Children*. We will now examine the demographics of these four shows in order to show how the audience has changed over in ten years.[1]

The audiences in 1971 and 1981 for both *The Guiding Light* and *As the World Turns* consisted mainly of older women. For both shows, approximately one-half of all women viewers over 18 were over 50. Also, the teenage audience was small in both years. Only 6 percent of the total *Guiding Light* audience was between 12 and 17, and a mere 4 percent of the *As the World Turns* audience were teenagers. A comparison with the 1981 figures shows almost no change. Both *The Guiding Light* and *As the World Turns* still attract many older viewers and few teenagers. The proportion of males in the audience has also increased slightly. In 1971, 16 percent of all viewers over 18 were male; in 1981, that proportion grew to close to 20 percent for both shows, reflecting the increased number of retired men and the loss of younger women under 49 who are presumably working outside the home or watching other soap operas.

In contrast, there are significant differences between the audiences for *General Hospital* and *All My Children* in 1971. *General Hospital* changed its orientation in 1977, and this change was clearly reflected in its audience. However, even in 1971 there were fewer older men and more teenagers viewing in comparison to the programs discussed earlier. Almost 9 percent of the 1971 audience was between 12 and 17, and only 35 percent were 50 and over, showing that *General Hospital,* even when it was considered more staid, managed to attract a younger audience. From its inception in 1970, *All My Children* has attracted youth and younger women. The demographics for that show in 1971 are unusual compared to the other soap operas: 10 percent of the total audience was between 12-17, and 30 percent over 50. In 1981, the differences between *As the World Turns* and *The Guiding Light* on the one hand, and *General Hospital* and *All My Children* on the other hand, are even clearer. *General Hospital's* adolescent audience rose to 15 percent, and the older, over-50 audience declined to 23 percent. The adolescent audience for *All My Children* actually declined slightly compared to 1971 (8 percent in 1981), as did the over-50 audience, down from 30 to 18 percent. *All My Children* should be a favorite with advertisers. Of all the shows analyzed, it attracts the largest proportion of women between 18 and 49 — 67 percent, compared to *General Hospital's* 59 percent, *As the World Turns'* 41 percent, and *The Guiding Light's* 41 percent.

We did not analyze in depth the audiences' household income, nor the regions of the country where specific soap operas are the most popular. To discuss regions of the country with any authority, one would have to explore migration patterns and population shifts. Also, a comparative analysis of incomes is not meaningful without discussing inflation in detail. However, rating charts suggest that the soaps have viewers in all economic categories, but that most viewers remain in the lower and middle levels, as they were in 1970 and 1971 (Katzman, 1972).

This analysis is superficial, but some questions are answered. We show that certain soap operas are popular with teenagers (mostly girls and young women), and that although the number of women in the labor force has increased, women viewers are still the majority. Overall, the number of men in the audience is relatively small, only a few percentage points higher than in 1971, but in both 1971 and 1981, most men in the audience (regardless of the soap opera) were in the over-50 category, suggesting that the soaps have appeal for the retired, regardless of sex. Again, however, the ABC soaps attract more teenage boys than any of the others (see Nielsen Television Index, 1971, 1981).

Most audience surveys are cross-sectional, and as far as we can tell, no one has examined the audience over time, except for the Nielsen data. More analyses should be done on that rich source of information. Although Nielsen data are restricted, more universities are adding these data files to their archives. However, Nielsen data can never provide the information most social scientists would like to know. For example, soap viewers could go in and out of the audience depending on their work status and whether they have alternative viewing opportunities from cable TV and video-tape recorders. The soap opera developed and has prospered because the networks had a virtual monopoly over television programming. Now that there are more women working for wages and more opportunities for them as well as others to choose what they view, regardless of the time of day, simply measuring household viewing is limiting.

Soap operas provide a medium through which advertisers try to reach women. Essentially, their primary purpose is to attract women 18-49 years old. As of now, it serves that function admirably. Those soap operas which accomplish this better than others are the most profitable. Ratings are conducted for advertisers and are therefore limited to describing the demographic characters of the audience. They cannot answer the questions that interest social science researchers such as why people watch soaps and how (or if) soap opera viewing affects behavior.

WHY DO PEOPLE WATCH SOAPS?

The reports on ratings and demographics are very informative about the audience that views in households. As already noted, however, they can tell us nothing about who does not watch, nor can they tell us very much about the characteristics of the audience, such as their other interests. If we wish to know why and how soap opera viewers compare to others, we must ask different questions. Frank and Greenberg (1980) conducted a large-scale national survey to find out how people use their leisure time. Of paramount interest was the use of television. In their survey, they combined two traditions of research: (1) market segmentation, a technique used mostly in the field of marketing and (2) need and gratification research, which, as will be further explained, has been used primarily by sociologists (Blumler and Katz, 1974). By combining both traditions, Frank and Greenberg were able to report on how different markets use television and to explain some of the reasons for this use. Because they only speculate on the gratifications that people get from watching television or from using other media, we discuss that important topic in a later section of the chapter.

Frank and Greenberg (1980: 33) surveyed a national probability sample consisting of 1133 households where they interviewed all occupants 13 years and older, resulting in 2476 actual interviews. The respondents were questioned about their interests and needs, as well as how they use various media — television, books, magazines, and radio. Through the use of factor analysis, they classified people into four large categories and fourteen subcategories. As might be expected, their major finding was that interest patterns and sex of respondent are highly correlated.

According to their analysis, the entire sample viewed soap operas 3.64 times in the four-week period covered in the interview. This figure is an average. Of course, some people did not watch any soap operas, while others were heavy viewers.

Table 7.2 shows the average number of times the soap operas were viewed by the fourteen interest segments. These data in some ways complement the Nielsen data presented earlier. The groups that viewed the most frequently were those in the adult female concentration with elderly concerns or who were family- and home-centered, and those in the youth concentration who were not socially active, athletic, or interested in science and engineering. Although not obvious from the table above, those in the youth concentration were also likely to be female.

Frank and Greenberg (1980: 105) describe the Elderly Concerns group as follows:

> Oldest segment, high percentage of retirees, widowed, few children. Very few interests include religion and news and information. Focus on maintaining sense of social integration and belonging in absence of direct contact. Need to overcome loneliness and lift spirits. Low need for intellectual stimulus.

Those in the Home and Community segment (1980:109) were also more likely to be adult females, married homemakers who are home- and community-oriented. They have the highest needs for family ties and understanding others, while their needs for intellectual stimulation and creative accomplishments are low. Along with soap operas, this group are heavy viewers of religious programs. Of this

TABLE 7.2 Average Number of Times Viewed by Interest Segment for Soap Operas

	Adult Male Concentration				Adult Female Concentration				Youth Concentration				Mixed		
	Entire Population	Mechanics and Outdoor Life	Money and Nature's Products	Family and Community Centered	Elderly Concerns	Arts and Cultural Activities	Home and Community Centered	Family Integrated Activities	Competitive Sports and Science/Engineering	Athletic and Social Activities	Indoor Games and Social Activities	News and Information	Detached	Cosmopolitan Self-Enrichment	Highly Diversified
Total	3.64	.92	2.81	1.20	7.13	2.77	6.56	5.32	1.05	3.12	5.59	5.11	3.61	.93	4.63
All My Children	.41	.20	.18	.09	.54	.35	.70	.89	.11	.50	1.10	.43	.36	.17	.29
Another World	.33	.10	.20	.09	.60	.21	.52	.39	.12	.27	.43	.48	.34	.19	.63
As the World Turns	.40	.07	.52	.26	1.07	.28	.70	.34	.09	.38	.37	.73	.31	.11	.39
Days of Our Lives	.37	.15	.20	.20	.77	.39	.72	.45	.16	.15	.49	.41	.30	.08	.53
The Doctors	.27		.28	.14	.56	.17	.44	.30	.07	.12	.27	.42	.31	.04	.57
General Hospital	.30	.01	.23	.09	.40	.23	.84	.64	.09	.26	.36	.36	.30	—	.24
The Guiding Light	.27	.05	.30	.07	.62	.22	.43	.19	.10	.42	.26	.59	.21	.10	.38
Love of Life	.27	.07	.17	.07	.64	.12	.44	.40	.09	.13	.48	.34	.43	.04	.26
One Life to Live	.32	.12	.14	.04	.46	.26	.67	.66	.07	.25	.89	.26	.27	.02	.40
Search for Tomorrow	.34	.06	.34	.06	.76	.22	.60	.42	.09	.21	.41	.61	.41	.06	.42
The Young and the Restless	.37	.10	.24	.09	.71	.32	.49	.64	.04	.42	.53	.49	.36	.12	.53

Source: Frank and Greenberg (1980). Reprinted by permission.

group, 35 percent are homemakers who are relatively cut off from adult companionship during the day and find that soap operas, game shows, religious programs, and talk shows satisfy a need for social integration.

The third group of heavy soap opera viewers are in the youth category, including those who are interested in indoor games and social activities. Again, this group is mostly female. Frank and Greenberg (1980: 117) describe them as young, low-income females with little interest in most subject matters and generally nonintellectual. They watch a substantial amount of television. In terms of average hours per week, individuals in this segment are 14 percent above the average. In comparison to members of the "Athletic and Social Activities" segment, also mostly young women, they are far more likely to watch television. In addition to being heavy viewers of soap operas and other daytime television, they also watch situation comedies and youth-oriented programs such as *Soul Train* and *American Bandstand*. That group consists of 21 percent black viewers, which no doubt accounts for their high interest in programs featuring black performers (Frank and Greenberg, 1980: 119).

Soap opera viewing is lowest among those segments with intellectual interests (also in the Adult Female Concentration) and among segments that are heavily populated with males. For example, as the chart shows, those in the segment labeled Mechanics and Outdoor Life, almost entirely male, and those labeled Cosmopolitan Self-Enrichment, consisting of equal proportions of men and women, view the soap operas the least.

Turning now to the number of college students who watch soap operas, only those who live at home or whose households were surveyed were included. However, from the survey data reported here and from the Nielsen data, a great deal has been learned.

The soap opera audience is obviously small when compared to the prime-time audience. That audience has been and remains predominantly female. However, even among the female soap opera audience, various segments or markets can be discerned — taste publics, as the sociologists have suggested (Gans, 1974; Lewis, 1981). There are clusters of people with common characteristics who pursue common activities, including soap opera viewing or nonviewing. For example, one cluster of soap opera viewers is elderly, another young. Not only do these two groups watch different soap operas, but they have different interest and taste patterns. There does, however, appear to be a high correlation between soap opera viewing and low involvement with intellectual pursuits or with activities involving crafts, mechanics, and sports. Whether the college audience makes up a different segment with different interests and activities is not known. The limited data gathered in the classroom (ABC, n.d.) suggest that college students who watch soap operas fit none of the categories developed by Frank and Greenberg, although they too are likely to be female.

Frank and Greenberg (1980) also present explanations for why people watch that vary from one audience segment to another. For example, they say that older women watch soap operas because they provide surrogate friends for people who spend a great deal of time at their sets, and that home-oriented viewers watch because they are relatively cut off from adult companionship during the day and thus use the soaps to satisfy their need for social integration. No explanation is given to account for so much viewing among the youth category, but the fact that they have little interest in intellectual subject matters implies that these young people are more limited in resources than others. We are not denying that explanation, but because no one has fully investigated the various segments among soap opera viewers, we remain limited in the generalizations that we make. The survey, although valuable, still does not fully answer the question of why people watch television. Frank and Greenberg provide even less information about what gratification viewers receive from watching, yet these two issues have concerned researchers for decades.

Uses and Gratifications

Most of the information as to why people watch prime-time television comes from researchers studying uses and gratifications (Blumler and Katz, 1974), but why people watch soap operas still lies almost wholly in the realm of speculation and prejudice. For example, McAdown (1974: 95) ascribed a sexual appeal to the soap operas, claiming that the audience dreams of their "union with the Buddha principle of the soaps: the ultimate doctor-dynamic which gently and knowingly fills their expectant recesses," to "guide the powerless safely through the ugly, smelly, bloody vagaries and complication of the life of the human female." Philip De-Muth and Elizabeth Barton (1982: 74) say that soaps "appeal to the sadomasochistic voyeurism that is one motivation behind soap-opera viewing. In Rome, it was the Colosseum; today it's *Another World.*"

It is widely accepted that the members of the soap opera audience are intellectually limited and watch soaps because they are socially isolated, lonely, and/or emotionally deprived. Frank and Greenberg's (1980) conclusions reported above support that generalization, as does some earlier research. For example, Helen Kaufman (1944) found segments among radio listeners, as reported earlier in the chapter, who were also intellectually and emotionally deprived, though she also found segments that did not fit that description. The most commonly cited research on the radio audience was conducted by Herta Herzog (1944), who reported three major reasons for listening to radio soaps: (1) emotional release — they give the listener a chance to cry or to feel better, knowing that others have problems too; (2) wishful thinking — they fill gaps in the listeners' own lives or compensate for failures; and (3) advice — practical explanations of appropriate patterns of behavior, useful when confronted with various life situations. Herzog and Kaufman used the same data for their analyses, and therefore Herzog also reports that listeners tended to be less educated and more

likely to live in rural areas than nonlisteners, though of similar income and age.

In a more recent study, Jay Blumler and his colleagues
(1970) interviewed listeners of *The Dales,* a British radio soap.
Their work also suggests that soap operas provide certain
gratifications for their listeners. They found six clusters of
gratifications that listeners derived from listening to *The
Dales.* The first cluster, personal reference, included statements such as: "The programme reminds me that I could be
worse off than I am." The second cluster, reality exploration,
is similar to the first, with items such as: "It sometimes helps
me to understand what is happening in my own life." The
chief difference between the first and second clusters is that
the second focuses on the exploration of problems. The third
cluster is based on reinforcement of family values: "It's nice
to know there are families like the Dales around today." A
fourth cluster, companionship, includes items such as: "I can
share in the happiness and sorrows of the characters." The
fifth cluster's core is what they call "a specific view of the
social role of women," one that favors maintaining decent
standards in the use of language and violence. The last cluster is about emotional release, including items such as:
"Sometimes it makes me want to cry," although few listeners
cited that last item as a gratification (Blumler et al., 1970: 14).

Blumler and his colleagues also found relationships between demographic characteristics and these gratifications,
so that some were more important for some segments of
viewers and some less important. Because all people in the
sample were followers of *The Dales,* we cannot generalize to
other programs or apply these findings to other sorts of
radio/television content.

From the early work on radio serials, it seems that listeners use soap operas to fulfill certain needs centered around
companionship and entertainment, personal reality exploration and, perhaps, emotional release. Blumler's (1978) later
work with other television content forms shows slightly different factors emerging that have little to do with personal

identity gratifications. These different factors could reflect a difference in the needs fulfilled by serials in comparison with other forms of television or radio, but that possibility has not been addressed directly in uses and gratification research.

Many studies of audience use and gratification suffer from the same difficulty. There are almost no studies comparing the gratifications that people receive watching different programs, and few studies on the gratifications received from viewing television soap operas. One such study was conducted by Ronald Compesi (1977), who studied viewers of *All My Children*. He developed a questionnaire using some of Herzog's and Blumler et al.'s work, as well as statements developed from pretesting *All My Children* viewers. The research protocol consisted of 52 gratification statements preceded by: "I like to watch *All My Children* because . . . "

Through factor analysis of the sample's responses to these statements, Compesi found that the most important gratification that viewers derived from the program was entertainment. Respondents said: "It's fun to watch." Following entertainment were habit ("I'm hooked on it") and convenience ("It's on at a convenient time"). The fourth most important reason for viewing was what Compesi called "social utility," reflected in such statements as: "I like to talk about the program with my friends." A less important gratification was relaxation and escape from problems ("It helps me to relax and release tension").

The Compesi sample differed in responses from those in both Herzog's and Blumler's early radio studies. The *All My Children* viewers did not find the program particularly useful socially for either advice or for increased understanding of their own lives. Compesi argues that the *All My Children* audience might be more sophisticated than the radio audiences. His sample was better educated than those in the earlier studies, and more educated viewers might consider a soap opera's attempt at social realism to be rather transparent. It could be argued, of course, that educated viewers might also be less likely to admit that they use soap operas for advice. It is also probable that television viewers today are more worldly about the media than they were when radio was young.[2]

The first three gratifications listed by Compesi — entertainment, habit, and convenience — are universal reasons for watching television, though they explain little about why a viewer would choose to watch daytime serials (or a particular serial) as opposed to other programs on television. The fourth factor, social utility, does suggest an explanation for some viewing. The dominant statement of the social utility factor in the Compesi study was: "I like to talk about the program with my friends." Another statement included in that cluster was: "My friends and I like to try and see who can figure out what will happen on the program." Clearly, the viewing of soaps is socially useful as a source of conversation but some thinking activity is also implicit in this process. Thus, part of the soaps' appeal for some viewers may be that audience members can be actively involved in the shows.

Blumler (1978) has recently argued that researchers need to shift the uses and gratifications approach slightly and should question empirically whether audience members are truly active. He also suggests that some media invite more activity than others.[3] One could further suggest that audience members might be more or less active depending on what program they were viewing. Certain types of content, such as daytime serials, might invite more and different kinds of activity than others, such as prime-time series.

A recent study by Suzanne Pingree (1981) tested directly for differences in viewer activity between soap operas and prime-time programming. Respondents to a telephone survey about daytime and prime-time viewing were asked about their degree of attention to various aspects of television programs, their recall and involvement with events, and how frequently they discussed television programs with others.

Most of the respondents who watched daytime television also watched prime-time programs as well, when their viewing activities were remarkably similar to those who watched only prime time. Except for a larger proportion of women, these soap/prime-time viewers were also demographically similar to those who watched only prime time. Differences in activity behavior between daytime serial viewing and prime-time viewing were clear, significant, and striking. Nearly every measure of activity used revealed that soap opera viewers are more active. For example, respondents were asked to name a television character who had recently done something they disliked. Soap opera viewers were better able to comply, a finding that was statistically significant. These viewers provided more specific information about the incident they recalled and responded with more emotion in their voice. A closer analysis of the answers given for prime-time programs suggests that the observed differences in activity behavior would have been even stronger had *Dallas* been counted as a daytime serial. Most people thought of J. R. Ewing when they recalled an incident involving someone they disliked on prime time.

Pingree's findings suggest that *the same people* view soap operas differently than prime-time programs, though they act similarly to those who do not watch soaps when they watch prime-time shows. We consider these findings to be very important, since they strongly suggest that program content accounts for some of the variability in viewers' activity. Because the same viewers are not active when they watch prime-time television, we believe that the soaps induce greater activity among the audience. This finding provides some evidence for our contention that all television effects are not the same, elaborated later in this chapter.

We do not yet have an answer to the question asked in the beginning of this section: Why do people watch soap operas? We do know that soaps are appealing and that they are more likely to generate active participation among viewers than other types of television, but more comparative studies need to be done to find out what soap operas mean to their viewers. Our approach in these last two sections was sociological; in the next one, a more psychological and individual approach is presented as we consider the behavioral and attitudinal effects that soap operas have on their audiences. Both are important for understanding the role of soaps for their audiences.

EFFECTS ON BEHAVIOR

Here we address the questions asked by most communication researchers: What effects do soap operas have on behavior, and how do soaps contribute to viewers' conceptions of reality that flow logically from the kinds of content discussed in Chapter 5.

Social and Interpersonal Relationships

A striking and robust characteristic of all soap operas is their focus on interpersonal relationships, especially interpersonal problems. For example, the divorce rate among serial characters is very high — almost half of all soap characters have been divorced. Thus, we could speculate that soap viewing might affect viewers' marital relations. People might be more apt to make small marital problems into big ones and consider divorce more readily than nonviewers. Marital partners might argue more as a result of viewing soaps. Of course, the opposite might be possible as well, since viewers could also respond to the same content reactively. Seeing relationships and marriages dissolve over misunderstandings and inappropriate behaviors may strengthen viewers' real-world relationships. Perhaps some viewers learn from soap characters' mistakes and avoid making similar mistakes in their own lives. Others might adopt strategies that soap characters used effectively or discard strategies that did not help to solve problems concerning their own interpersonal relationships. These viewing effects, if they happen at all, would have to happen unconsciously. All of the recent research of why people choose to watch, as we documented in the previous section, suggests very clearly that people do *not* watch soaps in order to get ideas about how to work out their own problems (see note 2).

Labor Force Participation

Soap viewing could be responsible for encouraging some women to enter the labor force. Soaps, more than any other genre of television, seem to have a strong work ethic and a strong career ethic emphasizing professional, high-status goals, and some soap opera women have always been part of the labor force, on radio as well as television. Thus viewing the soaps might encourage women to take on the extra hassles and risks of developing a career for themselves. Of course, those who do so would probably cease to be soap viewers, since it is difficult to pursue a career and still be home during the hours when the soaps are broadcast.[4]

The specific difficulties that many women face upon entering the work force — such as quality childcare and a double load of work, both at home and at the workplace — are rarely the subject of soap conflicts, though soap operas do pay attention to work-related threats to marital relationships. Women who are too dedicated to their careers — those willing to work at the expense of time with their spouses and/or children — often pay dearly for their ambition. Thus, soap viewers may be better prepared for marital problems than the day-to-day problems of careers.

Illnesses, Accidents, and Violence

It is difficult to imagine the effects on behavior of seeing characters who are ill with bizarre diseases or who are involved in accidents and/or murders. Perhaps soap viewers are more likely to be hypochondriacs than nonviewers, or maybe they drive less frequently, or stay indoors more to

avoid possible accidents or homicide attempts. Nevertheless, story themes probably affect attitudes and beliefs more
than behavior.

Another potential effect of watching soap operas could
be increased aggressive behavior. Although soaps do not
show as much violence as prime-time dramas, they do
present a picture of the world that is clearly more violent
than crime statistics suggest. However, should we find a
relationship between watching soaps and aggressive behavior, we would still be unsure whether it was a soap opera
effect or the result of watching other kinds of television.
Prime-time television is much more violent than the soaps,
and most soap viewers also watch prime-time programs. Any
relationship found could be due to the prime-time viewing
rather than watching the soaps.

In addition to statistically controlling for all other television viewing, we should consider the different kinds of effects that soap operas may have on aggressive behavior.
Because the soaps and prime time present violence differently, these differences could be used to discern the specific
kinds of aggressive behavior that soap viewing may precipi-
tate in comparison to prime-time viewing. For example,
soap viewing might cause verbal aggression and prime-time
viewing, physical aggression. It is also possible that female
viewers behave more aggressively because they are more
involved with soap operas but remain largely unaffected by
prime-time shows because they are less involved with them.
It might also be that any aggression caused by soap viewing
would be centered on interpersonal relationships, while that
caused by prime-time viewing would involve business,
money, or power.

Sex and Behavior

Soap operas, as we have noted, show more sexual incidents than prime-time dramas, and these incidents differ in
each kind of program. Therefore, there may be different

effects from viewing soaps than from prime-time viewing. Soap operas may be stimulating people to engage in sexual activities more frequently. We know that the soaps present a mixture of different types of sexual incidents, a large proportion of which involve petting between married individuals, and another portion of which is made up of references to intercourse between unmarried individuals. We might expect to find increases in both kinds of activity as a result of soap viewing. In contrast, prime-time viewing might have a more limited effect and only encourage sexual activity between unmarried partners (this being the most common portrayal on evening television).

Methodological Strategies

From the preceding discussion, it is obvious that we are unclear on how viewing affects individual behavior. Moreover, few researchers have addressed such questions as specifically as we have here. We believe that it is crucial to be specific — the more specific we are about the content of soaps and how that content is similar to and different from other television programs, the better our chances of isolating the effects of soap opera viewing. By using this type of approach, we have implicitly proposed a way to think about media effects in general. It is possible for researchers to analyze the content of soaps objectively, to measure exposure to the programs analyzed, and finally to assess the specific impact of soaps as a result of this exposure. The model of research being proposed is a traditional one that has been elaborated and changed over the years in mass media research. Included in the model are other factors that could alter the effects of television, such as the environmental, situational, and psychological characteristics of individual viewers. In other words, most mass communication researchers do not assume that television is all-powerful. Most effects research considers the important contributions to variations in people's behavior made by life experiences and other demographic characteristics, as well as more psychologically oriented factors, such as their reasons for using the media and how they feel about themselves. In any case, television is probably not a major determinant of behavior. At best, its influence is limited.

There are other possible effects of television viewing that may be independent of content. On one hand, it may be that the sound and picture movement raise the levels of noise and tension in households, thus leading to more arguments and dissension. On the other hand, television viewing makes some people very passive, inducing lethargy and even sleep. For some viewers it has a soothing effect in the sense that Wilbur Schramm (1971) describes — that is, that the mass media serve a "social radar" function by showing that the everyday business of the world is proceeding normally. There may also be interaction effects, in that family members who do not watch may still be affected by another member's involvement with certain programs. These possible effects, and in fact all such behavior effects, are purely speculative. There have been no studies on the behavioral effects of soaps, except for one questionable investigation of the relationship between suicides on the soaps and suicides in the larger society (see Phillips, 1982, and Kessler and Stipp, 1982), and only a few studies on how soaps affect attitudes, beliefs, and knowledge.

ADDITIONAL EFFECTS

Although we know that in comparison to their treatment of interpersonal problems, soap operas do not spend much time on social issues, it is possible that viewers (more than nonviewers) are better informed about some social issues, especially those believed by soap writers to be more central to women's lives. Soaps generally share a didactic quality. Just as the medical examiner in the prime-time series *Quincy* delivers a lecture at some crucial point in the drama on some aspect of medical practice considered socially relevant, so do characters on soaps inform viewers about the frequency of incest, the sociological and psychological aspects of rape and spouse abuse, the dangers of eating disorders, and the psychological trauma caused by a mastectomy. Thus, it is possible that soap opera viewers are more aware than non-viewers of battered women's refuges, of the procedures involved in abortion, and/or the risks and treatment options associated with breast cancer. (On the less useful side, they may also know fictional nonsense about amnesia and other common soap diseases that few will ever have.)

Soap operas may also influence viewers' attitudes about themselves. Some viewers may feel that their own lives are dreary and unexciting after exposure to the intense problems and extravagant lifestyles of most soap characters. In contrast, others may believe more in their own abilities to understand others' problems through their extensive surrogate experiences. Two studies have investigated these areas, with (unfortunately) contradictory results. Nancy Buerkel-Rothfuss and Sandra Mayes (1981) questioned 290 students in an introductory communications class at a large southern university. Among the students surveyed, they found that heavier viewers were less likely to feel satisfied with their own lives and had lower self-concepts, believing that they were less intelligent, less poised, inferior, and less competent than their classmates. In contrast, Bradley Greenberg and his colleagues (1982) found no support for the notion that viewers feel less life satisfaction. They also investigated viewers' beliefs about their ability to give advice and found that heavier viewers did not believe that they were better able than nonviewers to cope with problems because of the information available on the soaps. This may be due to the fact that Greenberg et al. (1982) studied different kinds of people — they did telephone interviews with adult women at home during the day rather than with college students.

Viewing soap operas may also cause some to believe that all problems are people-related. As a result, soap viewers may tend to approach problems in their own lives with an interpersonal bias. Whereas nonviewers would be more likely to attribute a job loss to the economy or to sex/race discrimination, viewers might assume that personality conflicts or other personal attributes were responsible. Although there have been no studies on how viewers personalize the problems on soap operas, there has been some research on a related effect. The soaps' concentration on interpersonal problems could influence viewers to believe that such problems are widespread and occur frequently. However, when Greenberg and his colleagues (1982) questioned adult women as to the severity of such problems as bad marriages, poor health, illicit love affairs, and divorce in this country today, they found little difference between soap viewers and others. Soap viewers were no more likely than nonviewers to say that these problems were serious.

Cultivation

One important topic in mass media research is the extent to which television influences viewers' concepts of social reality. George Gerbner and Larry Gross (1976) argue that television is the central cultural arm of American society, serving to socialize most people (especially children) into standardized roles and behaviors. According to this perspective, television does not accomplish this function overtly, but rather through the presentation of basic assumptions about the way life is and what values are important. They suggest that television cultivates people's beliefs about how the world works more through the sum total of interactions, behaviors, and values present in television content than through finite attempts to persuade.

Gerbner, his colleagues, and other researchers have translated this approach into a search for regularities in television content. Several different kinds of programs have been content analyzed using this approach (see Chapter 5) wherein investigators compare television regularities with real situations. For example, acts of violence and the social demography (sex, race, occupations of characters) found in the programs being studied are compared to government statistics to see how the television world compares to the real world. Researchers then survey television viewers to see how close they believe the television world corresponds to the real one. (For a fuller treatment of the research in this area, see Hawkins and Pingree, 1981, 1982.)

Following the cultivation perspective, Buerkel-Rothfuss and Mayes (1981) asked students they surveyed how often they viewed soaps (the number of episodes of each serial watched in a typical week), questioned them about their own life satisfaction, and asked them to make a number of estimates about issues relevant to soap content. For example, they asked the students to estimate the number of females out of every ten who would fit the following descriptions: are doctors, are lawyers, are housewives, do not work at all, have had an affair, are divorced, have had illegitimate children, have had abortions, and are happily married. Similar questions were asked about males.

After statistically controlling for age, grade point average, class standing, sex, and self-concept, Buerkel-Rothfuss and Mayes (1981) found moderate relationships between exposure to soaps and many of these estimates. They found that the more people watched soaps, the higher their estimates of the number of doctors and lawyers for both women and men, of businessmen, and of men and women who have had affairs, been divorced, and who have had illegitimate children. Heavier soap viewing was also associated with higher estimates of the number of women who are housewives, who have had abortions, who do not work at all, and of the number of people who have been divorced, been in jail, committed serious crimes, and who are happy. In addition, they found that people who watched more soaps tended to be less satisfied with their lives and to have lower self-concepts. Based on these findings, Buerkel-Rothfuss and Mayes (1981: 114) argue: "There appears to be an important relationship between what a person watches on daytime serials and what he or she believes to be true about those aspects of the 'real world' which tends to be portrayed with exaggerated frequency on soap operas."

However, they also point out that exposure to prime-time television might partially explain these relationships. As we stated earlier in the section on effects on behavior, most soap viewers also watch prime-time television. Unless we sort out the separate contribution of prime-time television's messages, we cannot be sure as to whether or not people are getting these messages from the soaps or from prime time.

In another cultivation study that used estimates about professional occupations and lifestyles to measure effects, Carveth and Alison (1982) found that prime-time television viewing was related to more of these beliefs than soap opera viewing. They found that heavy prime-time viewers thought there were more female lawyers, male and female doctors, people committing serious crimes, and males with illegitimate children. Watching soaps was related to only two beliefs: more male lawyers and more females with illegitimate children. Regarding these kinds of questions, focused on what must be described as the incidental content of television, it appears as though soap operas are contributing only a small amount of information to viewers' beliefs and are probably not as important as prime-time television.

It is possible, within the cultivation framework, to go beyond questions about the bits and pieces of incidental information with which viewers might construct a social reality. It may also be that these patterns of demography and action themselves imply values and ideologies. We know that there are explicit ideological/value statements made on soaps that might encourage viewers to infer meanings from these patterns. If viewers do make such inferences, soap operas could be leading them to construct a fairly traditional and conventional value system. For example, because so many of the interactions that occur on soaps are family-centered (spouses, parent-child, and so forth), viewers may come to believe that families are to be regarded as centrally important. Soap viewers may thus place great importance on the family and see it as the only place to live. Two studies provide evidence about this kind of effect.

Suzanne Pingree, Sandy Starrett, and Robert Hawkins (1979) mailed questionnaires to adult women about television viewing and beliefs about the family. They found that heavy soap viewers did seem to have a "family-as-good" value system, while this value system did not seem to be related to prime-time television. A second study with a larger sample consisted of a telephone survey by Pingree and Rouner (1982). It did not support this finding. In fact, the authors found the opposite: that there was no effect of soaps, and that heavy prime-time television viewers disagreed with the "family-as-good" perspective. However, this relationship depended on how the television was being watched. Where viewers were paying a lot of attention, where they were involved with the characters or programs, or said that they talked about the programs later with friends, there was no relationship between viewing and beliefs about the family. It seems, then, that the viewing situation itself — the quality of viewing — may be as important as the amount of viewing.

Implications for Research

It should be clear from our brief discussion of the research on beliefs, attitudes, and knowledge, that there is much more that can and should be done. We have not tried to be exhaustive here in what we have covered, but rather to stimulate thinking about how soaps (and television in general) might be influencing viewers.

Most research on television effects is based on a rather simplistic assumption: The more people are exposed, the more they will be affected. Traditionally, researchers have measured "exposure" by the number of hours spent per day watching television. It is difficult if not impossible to measure exposure accurately (a common mass communication problem). In addition, viewers themselves vary on whether they consider themselves, specifically, as part of the soap opera audience. Some consider themselves viewers if they watch once a month, while others watch every day. There may be what Greenberg and his colleagues (1982) call a "threshold effect." As they point out: "One can argue that effects, if they are to occur, may as well occur from a moderate amount of exposure which serves to establish a perceptual set toward a particular program and set of characters." They argue that after watching a soap just long enough to decide to continue watching it, though not necessarily on a daily basis, the impact on the viewer in terms of perceived realism and involvement may have already been achieved. Further watching may only maintain perceptions, not intensify them. They claim (and we agree) that magnitude of exposure then becomes a poor measure of outcome. Most soap opera viewers do not watch every day, while most prime-time viewers do. Clearly, the threshold effect of soaps ought to be studied. It is one of the specific methodological problems that must be addressed, particularly when studying soap effects.

In addition, any careful examination of soap operas shows that all soaps are not alike. They may be more similar to each other than prime-time series, which include several kinds of programs (sit-coms, police shows, family series, and others), but soaps are still remarkably dissimilar. Marilyn Fine's (1982) study illustrates this point. She studied conversations on *General Hospital* and several other daytime serials and found that the *General Hospital* conversations were markedly shorter, tended to involve no more than two people, and were more often about business than in other soaps. Several student research projects have also documented significant differences among the soaps. For example, one project found that CBS soaps had more discussions about sex and romance, while ABC soaps had more physically explicit references to sex. Another project analyzed the passage of time across several soaps and found that over the course of a week, two CBS soaps had yet to complete a full 24-hour period in their story lines, despite the fact that a holiday (Memorial Day) came and went in the period, while two ABC soaps completed nearly three full days in the same amount of time.

These examples are presented to illustrate that soaps carry different messages and present different social realities — that is, some show more women in professional occupations, while others show more sex. These differences illustrate the importance of specifically measuring *what* people watch, as well as how much they watch, when studying the effects of television. As we showed earlier in this chapter, most people in the audience do not watch all the soap operas. Without a video-tape recorder and several more available hours per day than most of us have, it is impossible to watch all of them. Most soap viewers regularly watch only a few and thus are being exposed to the messages peculiar to those few.

People cannot watch everything that is available on prime time, either. Moreover, prime-time television is an even more varied collection of different messages. We believe that the more specific we are about what people watch and the content of those programs, the more likely we are to be able to measure all kinds of effects.

When we look for effects, we tend to inquire as to whether viewers act in certain ways or hold certain beliefs that seem logically compatible with soap opera (television) content. For example, we expect to find people who are heavily exposed to sex-typed portrayals developing more rigid beliefs about the proper roles for themselves and others. The assumption behind this model is one of passivity (the "hypodermic model"). According to the model, audiences are receivers of information sent out by the mass media. Even when that formula is modified to take into account the "active" (or obstinate) characteristics of individuals, such as their life experiences, peculiar situations, and psychological needs, the hidden bias of the model is still that of a passive audience which accepts, under some conditions and in some situations, the message.

We know that soap audiences behave more actively with soaps than with other kinds of television. Whatever this activity means, it seems to be in conflict with the "passive audience assumption," that any effects will be isomorphic with television content. With an active, thinking audience bias, we might predict a wholly different kind of effect, one that is much more individual. If people are really thinking about what they are seeing, as soap viewers say they do, then we will probably be unable to predict their ultimate behavior, attitudes, or beliefs. We need to rethink what is meant by "effects" when the audience is active. Rather than being influenced, under some conditions and in some situations, the active audience is stimulated by television content. In fact, an active audience member might have a broader range of opinions, a better organized set of values and beliefs, and/or a more strongly held set of beliefs which center around issues and patterns present in television content when compared to those who do not view, or who view passively.

This review suggests a very different method for studying media effects, and one that ought to be considered for prime-time television as well. Individuals in the audience are not always passive when watching prime-time television, and they are not always active when watching the soaps. When audience members are inactive, perhaps the conventional model *is* appropriate. When they are active, however, different measures are needed to measure different kinds of effects. We should be able to test for the possibility that activity generates a different effect in order to ensure that the biases of our "effects" models match the behavior of the audience.

CONCLUDING REMARKS

Two elements stand out from this review of soap opera audiences. The most important one is that based on the data collected, whether from the Nielsen surveys, Frank and Greenberg (1980), uses and gratification studies, or the original research included here, there is not one audience for the soaps but several, depending on how audiences are conceptualized. Some may be emotionally deprived or isolated, but most are probably not, instead using soap operas as a means of social integration, talking and thinking about them with family and friends. However, because there are so few studies, there are no definitive conclusions about how the soaps affect their viewers.

The second element is that no one has addressed the question of how soap operas affect consciousness, especially feminist consciousness. What is on the soaps should be considered seriously, as we have emphasized, but what is *not* on them should also be considered. Feminists have argued (with some justification) that although the soaps are women's fiction, they present a very conservative view of the world. This view is derived not only from what is shown, but also from what is omitted, including such political issues as the Equal Rights Amendment. Such a perspective may affect women in ways that cannot be measured by social science methods but that may create an underlying socialization or cultivation effect from watching soaps (or reading women's fiction).

There is another issue that may be important. Viewing soap operas may be an effect in itself. Soap operas engage many viewers whose life circumstances are such that they are home during the daytime hours — housewives, the elderly and retired, and youngsters who find that schoolwork does not fill their time. That such viewers move in and out of the audience seems obvious but is rarely discussed. Viewers construct and reconstruct around these programs. Therefore, research needs to be more specific in considering life circumstances when studying the soap opera audience.

Throughout this chapter we have considered what soap operas do to viewers, but it also might be enlightening to turn that question on its head and ask how the audience affects the soaps. In the concluding chapter, that topic is briefly discussed as we speculate on the future of the soaps.

NOTES

1. *Days of Our Lives* and *The Guiding Light* were almost equal in ratings, with the latter only slightly lower, at 10.8, compared to *Days of Our Lives* at 11. We chose to compare *The Guiding Light* to the others because we are including the content analysis of that show over time (see Chapter 6).

2. Herta Herzog's study of how audiences use the soaps is the most widely quoted. Sometimes, recent researchers use her data as though they applied to contempory women, but in a personal conversation with her, she insisted that her findings ought to be put into historical perspective. She said that when radio was new, people were less sophisticated and more willing to take advice from radio characters than they might be now from television characters.

3. From the inception of television, it was noted that viewers "paid more attention" to daytime programs than to other kinds of television (Whan, 1958).

4. There are a number of idiosyncratic reports from viewers showing that in some workplaces, soap fans either watch during their lunch breaks or listen to the serials on special FM band radios that pick up the audio portion of the programs.

8

CONCLUSION

In this chapter, we summarize briefly how the soap opera has changed, speculate on its future, and discuss how the audience may affect the soap opera.

Throughout this book, the soap opera has been examined both as a form of popular culture directed at women and transmitted through commercial television, and as an economic commodity important to broadcasters for its profits. Soap operas are a unique form of entertainment, different from other television drama, although both are broadcast over the same networks. There are also subtle (but important) differences among the soap operas themselves, differences in format, content (expressive elements), and audience. Overall, the soaps differ from other program types, especially prime-time television, in their mode of production, content, and in the audiences they reach (as well those the creators want to reach).

The differences in content between prime-time and day-time television are directly tied to the differences in audience. Soap operas, along with sports programming, news broadcasts, and children's shows, all provide examples of programs easily recognized as targeted to special segments. Soap operas are especially significant because the target audience is women — not all women, but those home during the day who are between 18 and 49 years old. As that audience changed, so has the content of soap operas.

Both the form and content of the soaps have evolved to their present state partly because their certain advertisers and networks had originally wanted to reach housewives as consumers. As that key audience changed and new audiences were attracted, however, the content of the soaps also changed in subtle but important ways. Broadcasters adopted a profitable and popular literary form of the nineteenth and twentieth centuries, the domestic novel, and transformed it to fit the original target audience and later both the changing markets and the technology through which it was transmitted.

Soap operas have been broadcast for over fifty years, thirty years on radio and over thirty years on television. (For ten years, 1951-60, they were on both media.) The radio soap operas, especially those produced by Frank and Anne Hummert, were often melodramatic and, as some claim, naive and moralistic. However, those who have studied the radio soap opera seriously note that the serials varied substantially. For example, as early as 1944 researchers were reporting the differences between those soap operas that captured lower socioeconomic listeners as compared to those capturing more middle-class audiences (Kaufman, 1944).

By focusing on family and interpersonal relationships, television soap operas not only appear to be very much alike, but also to be more realistic than their predecessors. Many critics have failed to recognize that all soaps are not alike, that there are differences among them in content and style. The newer soaps — those introduced or changed fundamentally in the 1970s (for example, *All My Children* and *General Hospital*) — are more sensational and more likely to be concerned with "liberal" issues such as abortion, mental health, and child and wife battering, while the older soaps continue to focus primarily on family relationships.

Just as the problems of real life have changed over 50 years, so have the fictional presentations of the real world on soap operas. Of course, changes on a soap opera are subtle and not at all revolutionary. Unfortunately, most content analyses of the soaps are time-bound. Analysis of the radio soaps and of *The Guiding Light* scripts over 35 years indicate that the same phenomenon that Betty Friedan (1963) reported in magazine fiction may have occurred in the soaps, too. The Woman Alone theme in radio, where women were portrayed as doctors, lawyers, radio announcers, actors, and businesswomen, may have been superseded by the traditional housewife in the 1950s and 1960s as part of the general feminine mystique that followed World War II.

During the 1970s, more women in soap operas were portrayed in the labor force, and as the decade progressed, more were working in nontraditional occupations. However, whether earning wages or staying at home, the concerns of family and interpersonal relations have remained central, just as they were in the radio soaps. The difference is that the workplace as a setting is becoming equally as important as the home for personal interactions. Topics of conversation are also changing. The most obvious change in soap opera content has been in the area of sexual relationships and sexual morality, not in sex role portrayals. The radio soap opera stressed sexual purity, especially for women. Adultery was always clearly punished and virginity before marriage highly valued. Adultery and premarital sex are now prevalent on television soap operas, and the punishments for these recognized transgressions, although still present, are not as clear-cut as they once were. There are even examples of deviant behavior (for example, a rape on *General Hospital)* being rewarded.

In summary, the soap opera is far more complex than its critics would contend. There have been changes in the ways men and women are portrayed and in the ways they interact, although the soaps still remain a form of women's fiction where interpersonal problems, love, motherhood, family, and marriage take precedence over societal problems. Individual problems, mostly those traditionally defined as "feminine," remain central; those arguing that content does not change can show that certain themes and conditions recur again and again — amnesia, illness, career conflicts, upward mobility for women through marriage, and so forth. Producers and writers freely admit that they recycle plots, updating them to make them trendy. However, by introducing new ideas about sexual relations and work, the soaps, though conservative, reflect changing social conditions and changing audience structures, albeit imperfectly.

Those who create and finance soap operas — advertisers, networks, and the writers who work for those institutions — are attempting to reach 18-49-year-old women who consume household products, beauty aids, feminine hygiene products, and drugs. The audience they reach does include a large segment of those women, but that audience varies from soap opera to soap opera. The soap opera audience not only differs from the prime-time audience (although some people are members of both), but there are different audience segments among soap viewers. Some soap operas are more likely to attract the younger viewers (under 30), others older viewers (over 50). Both the Nielsen ratings and other surveys (Frank and Greenberg, 1980) show that although soap creators may prefer the 18-49-year-old housewife, they also get many older and younger viewers whom they are not making an effort to attract. This fact has not gone unnoticed by some producers, particularly those at ABC who have changed the content of their soaps in order to target younger women — a strategy that appears to be working. At the same time, the older viewers who remain at the core of other soap opera audiences seem satisfied with the content offered there.

Ratings and demographic studies tell us little about audience interest and involvement in particular programs, although a few studies have been conducted with soap audiences suggesting that they are more active and involved in these programs than are prime-time viewers. In addition, all soap opera actors and producers recognize and report anecdotally that there are some viewers who take the soaps a bit *too* seriously. Actors report how they are accosted by viewers on the street who cannot separate them as people from the roles they play. Producers report that they receive letters with advice to characters on child care, clothes selection, and other personal matters. The importance of the soap operas to these kinds of viewers cannot be overestimated.

Both interested viewers and ratings are powerful influences on the soaps. Interested viewers are powerful because producers and writers often have them in mind when repeating themes or persisting in presenting a relatively conservative view of the social world, and ratings because they determine the life, death, and sometimes the direction of particular shows. Although soap operas are not subject to the same trends and cycles associated with prime-time programs, they are still changed and can always be canceled. (Both *The Doctors* and *Texas* were dropped from the schedule as of the end of 1982 because of very low ratings.) Production companies will often give writers more leeway to innovate when ratings are low. Thus, the involved audience, although a vocal minority, may be the least powerful when networks and advertisers decide that a show is in trouble, but remain the reference audience for those who are working day to day on relatively successful shows. Although the writers and producers often make fun of the tendency of some audience members to confuse fiction with reality, these creators may also be writing specifically for them. Several admit that they often write with tongue in cheek, often showing disrespect for that audience segment, while others claim that they are educating the audience or providing "lessons for life." However, whether being cynical or sincerely trying to communicate didactic messages, writers, along with the production organizations, are all aware of their audience, that those whom they target and the majority of those they might reach are primarily (but clearly not all) female. Thus their conceptions of the female audience remain the essence of the soap opera as we know it.

THE FUTURE

As we write this book, broadcasting in America is changing so rapidly that it is difficult to write the final chapter. The soap, because it is so closely tied to network television, will no doubt change as the networks change. The two factors usually proposed as contributing to changes in broadcasting are the adoption of new technologies that allow viewers to make alternative use of their television sets, and the changing nature of the audience, reflecting new trends in work and leisure in the United States. There is no question that advertisers and network executives rely on ratings for decision making, aware that the audience for daytime (and prime-time) television has been shrinking throughout the 1970s and that it continues to shrink in the 1980s. The decision to continue their support of original daytime drama means that audience size is not always synonymous with profits. At this time, at least for daytime programming, audience composition (demographics) is more important than large numbers. One can only speculate as to whether the networks will continue their support of serial drama during the day if the target audience continues to decline.

As we become a more service- and information-oriented society, the daytime audience might increase as more work takes place in households, since viewing and working will occur in the same place. More people, both men and women, may also be working intermittently rather than continuously, performing work labeled "casual." (There are already indications that the number of casual workers in the United States is increasing.) During periods of unemployment, many people watch more daytime television, only to give up such viewing once they are newly employed. The fact that college students watch soaps provides an example of this phenomenon. No doubt most who were viewers as students do not view once they become employed. (Some, however, might continue as listeners on TV-band portable radios.) The older audience should also increase in the coming decade.

There is a great deal of evidence that the 18-49-year-old audience will continue to shrink as more women enter the labor force. Like other segments of the audience, members of that age group are increasingly able to choose alternative channels, including cable, pay TV, and UHF stations, as they become available. Also, at this particular moment in history the core audience for soap operas is large because of the baby boom following World War II. However, as a result of the substantial drop in the birth rate since 1955, the proportion of women between 18 and 49 will be declining. If the audience changes as predicted, the time of day will no longer determine the kinds of programs broadcast.

Both technology and the changing nature of work and leisure are important to the soap opera's future. For most Americans, television viewing is currently tied to the time of day when programs are offered. As George Comstock (1982a) has pointed out, the audience usually makes two decisions concerning their participation as viewers: when to watch and what to watch. For viewers who now own video-tape recorders, and for many more in the future, the only decision will be when to watch. Thus, workers will be able to watch soap operas (if they are still on the air), and those not in the work force will be able to select any program they wish.

If commercial television should change radically because it is no longer able to deliver audiences to advertisers, the soap opera as we know it could disappear. As of now (Spring 1983), however, ABC at least is still vigorously supporting daytime serials. A new soap has been scheduled to be launched in June 1983 on that network — *Loving*, created by Agnes Nixon and written by Douglas Marland (O'Leary, 1983; Farley, 1983). It is also probable that in the foreseeable future programs targeted to women will still be available, both soaps and their new competitors — romance mini-series and twice-weekly evening serials such as *A New Day in Eden,* produced by Lorimar, which also produces *Dallas* and *Knotts Landing*. Some social scientists are suggesting that, in view of the competition developing from video recorders and cable, such programming might also save commercial TV broadcasting in its present form (O'Leary, 1983).

From this study, we know that soap operas, as distinct from other dramatic programs, have a different history, a different mode of production, different (but overlapping) audiences, and different content. Because soap opera viewers are likely to be more involved with these programs when compared to those who view only prime-time programs, the effects of viewing are probably different as well. The soaps have been and continue to be an integral part of American culture for over fifty years. They engage millions of women (and some men) regularly. The messages they communicate, how they cultivate social reality, and what they mean to their audiences and to broadcasters should be a matter of concern to all who care about relationships between men and women and about the relationship of the media to individual behavior and societal change.

BIBLIOGRAPHY

ABC (n.d.) "They watching." ABC Daytime Serials, College Student TV Survey provided by American Broadcasting Co.

A. C. NIELSEN COMPANY (1978) The Nielsen Ratings in Perspective: A Description of the Media Research Services Group of the A. C. Nielsen Co. Northbrook, IL: Author.

ARNHEIM, R. (1944) "The world of the daytime serial," pp. 34-85 in P. Lazarsfeld and F. Stanton (eds.) Radio Research, 1942-1943. New York: Duell, Sloan and Pearce.

BARNOUW, E. (1978) The Sponsor: Notes on a Modern Potentate. New York: Oxford University Press.

———— (1975) Tube of Plenty. New York: Oxford University Press.

———— (1970) The Image Makers: A History of Broadcasting in the United States From 1953. New York: Oxford University Press.

———— (1968) The Golden Web: A History of Broadcasting in the United States, 1933-1953. New York: Oxford University Press.

———— (1966) A Tower of Babel: A History of Broadcasting in the United States to 1933. New York: Oxford University Press.

BAYM, N. (1978) Women's Fiction: A Guide to Novels By and About Women in America, 1820-1870. Ithaca, NY: Cornell University Press.

BERNARD, J. (1981) The Female World. New York: Free Press.

BLUMLER, J. (1978) "The role of theory in uses and gratification studies." Communication Research 6: 9-36.

———— and E. KATZ (1974) The Uses of Mass Communications. Beverly Hills, CA: Sage.

BLUMLER, J., J. R. BROWN, and D. McQUAIL (1970) "The social origins of the gratifications associated with television viewing." Unpublished.

Broadcasting (1981) "Census results in market changes." June 15.

———— (1977) "In search of those missing daytime viewers." November 7.

———— (1972) "Writing on: Irna Phillips mends with tradition." November 6.

BUERKEL-ROTHFUSS, N. with S. MAYES (1981) "Soap opera viewing: the cultivation effect." Journal of Communication 31: 108-115.

BUSBY, L. (1975) "Sex-role research on the mass media." Journal of Communication 25: 107-131.

Business Week (1979) "For network TV, a sudden case of future shock." October 29.

CANTOR, M. G. (1982) "The organization and production of prime-time television," pp. 349-362 in D. Pearl et al. (eds.) Television and Behavior: Ten Years of Scientific Progress and Implication for the Eighties. Washington, DC: Government Printing Office.

────── (1980) Prime-Time Television: Content and Control. Beverly Hills, CA: Sage.

────── (1979) "Our days and our nights on TV." Journal of Communication 29: 66-73.

────── (1971) The Hollywood TV Producer: His Work and His Audience. New York: Basic Books.

────── and E. JONES (1983) "Creating fiction for women." Communication Research 10: 111-137.

CANTRIL, H. (1940) The Invasion from Mars: A Study in the Psychology of Panic. Princeton, NJ: Princeton University Press.

CARVETH, R. and A. ALISON (1982) "Learning from television whether you intend to or not: reality exploration and the cultivation effect." Presented at the annual meetings of the Eastern Communication Association, Hartford, CT.

CASSATA, M.B., T.D. SKILL, and S.O. BOADU (1979) "In sickness and in health." Journal of Communication 29: 73-80.

COHN, D.L. (1943) Love in America. New York: Simon & Schuster.

COMPESI, R. (1980) "Gratifications of daytime TV serial viewers." Journalism Quarterly 57: 155-158.

────── (1977) "Reconsidering daytime serial audience gratifications: an analysis of fans of the program All My Children." Presented at the annual meetings of the Western Speech Communication Association, Phoenix.

COMSTOCK, G. (1982a) "Television and social institutions," pp. 334-348 in D. Pearl et al. (eds.) Television and Behavior: Ten Years of Scientific Progress and Implications for the Eighties. Washington, DC: Government Printing Office.

────── (1982b) "Violence in television content: an overview," pp. 108-125 in D. Pearl et al. (eds.) Television and Behavior: Ten Years of Scientific Progress and Implications for the Eighties. Washington, DC: Government Printing Office.

COMSTOCK, G., S. CHAFFEE, N. KATZMAN, M. McCOMBS, AND D. ROBERTS (1978) Television and Human Behavior. New York: Columbia University Press.

CRAFT, R. (1982) "Elegy for Mary Hartman," in H. Newcomb (ed.) Television: The Critical View. New York: Oxford University Press.

DeFLEUR, M.L. and S. BALL-ROKEACH (1982) Theories of Mass Communication (4th ed.). New York: Longman.

DEMUTH, P. and E. BARTON (1982) "Soap gets in your mind." Psychology Today 16 (July): 74-78.

DOWNING, M. (1974) "Heroine of the daytime serials." Journal of Communication 24: 130-137.

DUNNING, J. (1976) Tune-In Yesterday: The Ultimate Encyclopedia of Old-Time Radio, 1925-1976. Englewood Cliffs, NJ: Prentice-Hall.

EDMONDSON, M. and D. ROUNDS (1976) From Mary Nobel to Mary Hartman. New York: Stein & Day.

────── (1973) The Soaps. New York: Stein & Day.

FARLEY, E. (1983) "General Hospital at 20." Los Angeles Times, April 1, Part IV.

Federal Communications Commission (1980) Analysis of Television Program Production, Acquisition and Distribution. Washington, DC: Author.

FERNANDEZ-COLLADO, C.F. and B.S. GREENBERG, with F. KORZENNY and C.K. ATKIN (1978) "Sexual intimacy and drug use in TV series." Journal of Communication 28: 30-37.

FINE, M. G. (1982) "New suds, same soap." Presented at the annual meetings of the International Communication Association, Boston.

——— (1981) "Soap opera conversations: the talk that binds." Journal of Communication 31: 97-107.

FRANK, R. E. and M. G. GREENBERG (1980) The Public's Use of Television. Beverly Hills, CA: Sage.

FRANZBLAU, S., J. N. SPRAFKIN, and E. A. RUBINSTEIN (1978) A Content Analysis of Physical Intimacy on Television. New York: Brookdale International Institute.

FRIEDAN, B. (1963) The Feminine Mystique. New York: Dell.

GANS, H. J. (1974) Popular Culture and High Culture. New York: Basic Books.

GERBNER, G. (1972) "Violence in television drama: trends and symbolic functions," pp. 28-187 in G. A. Comstock and E. A. Rubinstein (eds.) Television and Social Behavior, Vol. 1. Washington, DC: Government Printing Office.

——— and L. GROSS (1976) "The scary world of TV." Psychology Today 9: 41-45.

GOLDSEN, R. (1977) The Show and Tell Machine: How Television Works and Works You Over. New York: Dial Press.

——— (1976) "Throwaway husbands, wives and lovers." Human Behavior 35 (December): 64-69.

GREENBERG, B. S. (1982) Life on Television. Norwood, NJ: Ablex.

——— R. ABELMAN, and K. NEUENDORF (1981) "Sex on the soap opera: afternoon delight." Journal of Communication 31: 83-89.

GREENBERG, B. S., K. NEUENDORF, N. BUERKEL-ROTHFUSS, AND L. HENDERSON (1982) "What's on the soaps and who cares?" Journal of Broadcasting 26: 519-536.

HAWKINS, R. P. and S. PINGREE (1982) "Television's influence on social reality," pp. 224-247 in D. Pearl et al. (eds.) Television and Behavior: Ten Years of Scientific Progress and Implications for The Eighties. Washington, DC: Government Printing Office.

——— (1981) "Using television to construct social reality." Journal of Broadcasting 25: 347-364.

HERZOG, H. (1961) "Motivations and gratifications of daily serial listeners," pp. 50-55 in W. Schramm (ed.) The Process and Effects of Mass Communication. Urbana: University of Illinois Press.

——— (1944) "What do we really know about daytime serial listeners?" pp. 3-33 in P. F. Lazarsfeld and F. Stanton (eds.) Radio Research, 1942-1943. New York: Duell, Sloan and Pearce.

HIGBY, M. J. (1968) Tune in Tomorrow. New York: Ace.

HIRSCH, P. M. (1977) "Television as a national medium: its cultural and political role in American society," in D. Street (ed.) Handbook of Urban Life. San Francisco: Jossey-Bass.

HOLSTI, O. (1969) Content Analysis for the Social Sciences and Humanities. Reading, MA: Addison-Wesley.

HOWER, R. M. (1949) The History of An Advertising Agency. Cambridge, MA: Harvard University Press.

INTINTOLI, M. (n.d.) "Making soaps: some initial observations on the making of a television daytime serial." Unpublished.

KATZ, E. (1977) Social Research on Broadcasting: Proposals for Further Development — A Report to the British Broadcasting Corporation. London: BBC.

KATZMAN, N. (1972) "Television soap operas: what's been going on, anyway?" Public Opinion Quarterly 36: 200-212.

KAUFMAN, H. (1944) "The appeal of specific daytime serials," pp. 86-110 in P. Lazarsfeld and Stanton (eds.) Radio Research, 1942-1943. New York: Duell, Sloan and Pearce.

KEELER, J. (1980) "Soaps: counterpart to the 18th century's quasi-moral novel." New York Times, March 16, p. 34.

KESSLER, R. C. and H. STIPP (1982) "The impact of fictional television suicide stories on U.S. suicides." Unpublished.

KINZER, N. S. (1977) Put Down and Rip Off. New York: Thomas Y. Crowell.

KOCH, H. (1970) The Panic Broadcast. New York: Avon.

KRIPPENDORF, K. (1982) Content Analysis. Beverly Hills, CA: Sage.

LACKMANN, R. (1976) TV Soap Opera Almanac. New York: Berkeley.

LAGUARDIA, R. (1977) From Ma Perkins to Mary Hartman: The Illustrated History of Soap Opera. New York: Ballantine.

——— (1974) The Wonderful World of Soap Operas. New York: Ballantine.

LAUB, B. [Ed.] (1977) The Official Soap Opera Annual. New York: Ballantine.

LeMAY, H. (1981) Eight Years in Another World. New York: Atheneum.

LEWIS, G. H. (1981) "Taste cultures and their composition: towards a new theoretical perspective," pp. 201-219 in E. Katz and T. Szecsko (eds.) Mass Media and Social Change. Beverly Hills, CA: Sage.

——— (1978) "The sociology of popular culture." Current Sociology 26 (Winter): special issue.

LISS, M. (1981) "Blind and deaf viewers: is one modality sufficient for comprehension?" Presented at the annual meetings of the Society for Research in Child Development, Boston.

LOPATE, C. (1976) "Daytime television: you'll never want to leave home." Feminist Studies 3: 69-82.

LOWRY, D. T., G. LOVE, and M. KIRBY (1981) "Sex on the soap operas: patterns of intimacy." Journal of Communication 31: 90-96.

MacDONALD, J. F. (1979) Don't Touch That Dial: Radio Programming in American Life from 1920 to 1960. Chicago: Nelson-Hall.

MANKIEWICZ, F. and J. SWERDLOW (1978) Remote Control: Television and The Manipulation of American Life. New York: Ballantine.

McADOWN, R. (1974) "Experiences of soap opera." Journal of Popular Culture 7: 955-965.

McCORMACK, T. (1982) "Content analysis: the social history of a method," in T. McCormack (ed.) Culture, Code, and Content: Communications Studies, Vol. II. Greenwich, CT: JAI.

——— (1981) "Male conceptions of female audiences: the case of soap operas." Presented at the International Interdisciplinary Conference on Women, Haifa, Israel, 28 December.

Media Probes (1981) "Soap operas," a production of Laybourne/Lambe, Inc. broadcast by the Public Broadcasting Service.

MEJIAS-RENTAS, (1982) "Soap en espanol." Los Angeles Times Calendar Section, Sept. 19.

MIES, D. (1982) "The Guiding Light — 1948-1982." M.A. thesis, University of Wisconsin-Madison.

NEWCOMB, H. (1981) "Texas: a giant state of mind." Channels 1.

—— (1974) TV: The Most Popular Art. New York: Doubleday.

—— and R. S. ALLEY (1982) "The producer as artist: commercial television," in J. S. Ettema and D. C. Whitney (eds.) Individuals in Mass Media Organizations: Creativity and Constraint. Beverly Hills, CA: Sage.

Newsweek (1981) "TV's hottest show." September 28.

Nielsen Television Index (1981) "National audience demographics: Monday-Friday daytime estimates of individual network program audiences." New York: A. C. Nielsen.

—— (1971) "NAC audience demographics report" (four weeks ending February 28). New York: A. C. Nielsen.

NIXON, A. E. (1970) "Coming of age in sudsville." Television Quarterly 9: 61-70.

O'LEARY, S. (1983) "The greatest stories ever told." Emmy Magazine, March/April.

People (1982) "Are soaps too sexy?" June 14.

PHILLIPS, D. P. (1982) "The impact of fictional television stories on U.S. adult fatalities: new evidence of the effect of the mass media on violence." American Journal of Sociology 87: 1340-1359.

PINGREE, S. (1981) "Audience activity with daytime and prime time television." Unpublished.

—— and D. ROUNER (1982) "The cultivation of family values with daytime serials." Unpublished.

PINGREE, S., S. STARRETT, and R. HAWKINS (1979) "Soap opera viewers and social reality." Unpublished.

RAVAGE, J. W. (1977) "Not in the quality business': a case study of contemporary television production." Journal of Broadcasting 21: 47-60.

REED, J-M. (1983) "The soaps." Los Angeles Times, Part V, p. 10.

RICHARDSON, S. (1740) Pamela: On Virtue Rewarded. (Many modern editions available.)

ROSE, B. (1979) "Thickening the plot." Journal of Communication 29: 81-84.

Ross Reports (1951) February-July, Vol. 16.

SANDEEN, C. A. and R. J. COMPESI (1981) "Central stylistic control in daytime television serial production: an analysis of The Young and The Restless." Presented at the annual meetings of the Western Speech Communication Association, October.

SCHRAMM, W. (1971) "The nature of communication between humans," in W. Schramm and D. F. Roberts (eds.) The Process and Effects of Mass Communication. Urbana: University of Illinois Press.

SEEGAR, J. and P. WHEELER (1973) "World of work on TV: ethnic and sex representation in TV drama." Journal of Broadcasting 17: 201-214.

SHOWALTER, E. (1977) A Literature of Their Own. Princeton, NJ: Princeton University Press.

SIEPMANN, C. A. (1950) Radio, Television, and Society. New York: Oxford University Press.

SIGNORIELLI, N. (1982) "The demography of the television world." Presented at the Symposium on Cultural Indicators for the Comparative Study of Culture, Vienna, February 16-19.

—— (1979) "Television's contribution to sex role socialization." Presented at the Seventh Annual Telecommunications Policy Research Conference, Skytop, PA, April.

SILVERMAN, L. T., J. N. SPRAFKIN, AND E. A. RUBINSTEIN (1978) "Sex on television: a content analysis of the 1977-78 prime-time programs." New York: Brookdale International Institute.

SOARES, M. (1978) The Soap Opera Book. New York: Harmony.

SPAULDING, J. W. (1979) "1918: radio becomes a mass advertising medium," pp. 70-81 in J. W. Wright (ed.) New York: Delta.

STEDMAN, R. W. (1977) The Serials: Suspense and Drama by Installments. Norman: University of Oklahoma Press.

———— (1959) "A history of the broadcasting of daytime serial dramas in the United States." Ph.D. dissertation, University of Southern California.

STEIN, B. (1979) The View from Sunset Strip. New York: Basic.

STRAUBHAAR, J. D. (1981) "Estimating the impact of imported versus national television programming in Brazil." Presented at the Conference on Culture and Communication, Temple University, Philadelphia, April 10.

STROTHERS, L. (1981) "The brown shadow syndrome: minority-majority relationships in daytime television serials. Unpublished.

SUTHERLAND, J. C. and S. J. SINIAWSKY (1982) "The treatment and resolution of moral violations on soap operas." Journal of Communication 32: 67-74.

TEDESCO, N. S. (1974) "Patterns in prime time." Journal of Communication 24: 119-124.

TEGLER, P. (n.d.) "The daytime serial: a bibliography of scholarly writings, 1943-1981." (unpublished)

THURBER, J. (1948) The Beast and Me. New York: The Hearst Corporation.

Time (1976) "Sex and suffering in the afternoon." January 12.

TUROW, J. (1974) "Advising and ordering: daytime, prime time." Journal of Communication 24: 138-141.

TUCHMAN, G. (1979) "Women's depiction in the mass media." Signs 4: 528-542.

———— (1978) Making News: A Study in the Construction of Reality. New York: Free Press.

TV Guide (1956) "Soap operas — and how they grew." August 10.

WAITE, L. J. (1981) "U.S. women at work." Population Bulletin 36 (May).

WAKEFIELD, D. (1976) All Her Children. New York: Avon.

Wall Street Journal (1979) "The decline of the weekly series." July 12.

WANDER, P. (1979) "The angst of the upper class." Journal of Communication 29: 85-88.

WARD, A. (1974) "How 'As the World Turns' turns: two days in the life of a soap opera." AFI Report 5: 28-34.

WARNER, W. S. and W. E. HENRY (1948) "Big sister." Genetic Psychology — supplement to Vol. 37.

WARRICK, R. (1980) The Confessions of Phoebe Tyler. Englewood Cliffs, NJ: Prentice-Hall.

WEIBEL, K. (1977) Mirror, Mirror: Images of Women Reflected in Popular Culture. New York: Anchor.

WHAN, F. L. (1958) "Special report: daytime use of TV by Iowa housewives." Journal of Broadcasting 2 (Spring: 142-148.

WILLEY, G. A. (1963) "The soap operas and the war." Journal of Broadcasting 7(4): 339-353.

———— (1961) "End of an era: the daytime radio serials." Journal of Broadcasting 5 (Spring): 97-115.

World Almanac (1982) New York: Newspaper Enterprise Association.

INDEX

ABOUT THE AUTHORS

MURIEL G. CANTOR, who received her Ph.D. in sociology from the University of California, Los Angeles, wrote her dissertation on the sociology of television producers, later published as *The Hollywood TV Producer.* Since that time, she has been investigating various aspects of television drama, how it is created, by whom, and under what conditions. Her published works on the subject have appeared in *Communication Research, Journal of Communication, Journalism Quarterly,* and several collections of readings. A recent book, *Prime-Time Television: Content and Control,* is also a Sage CommText publication. She has been a consultant for the corporation for Public Broadcasting, the National Institute of Mental Health, the U.S. Office of Education, and the National Organization for Women. In addition, she contributed to the Report to the Surgeon General on Television and Social Behavior in 1972 and to the update of that report, *Television and Behavior,* in 1982. She is currently Professor of Sociology at American University, Washington, D.C., where she was former Chair of the Department. During 1982, she was visiting Professor of Communication Studies at UCLA and she spent the first half of 1983 in London comparing British television soap operas to American.

SUZANNE PINGREE is an Assistant Professor in the Department of Agricultural Journalism and in the School of Family Resources and Consumer Sciences at the University of Wisconsin—Madison. She earned her Ph.D. in communication at Stanford University in 1975. She had been conducting research on the effects of television on children for almost ten years, and has published articles in most of the communication journals. Her research now focuses on active processes in television viewers' constructions of social reality. She has taught a summer course on soap operas since 1979.